# Understanding AI: A Comprehensive Guide for Beginners

Frank Zanish

# Contents

# Chapter One

# The AI Revolution

## Introduction to AI Impact

The world as we know it is rapidly changing, and at the heart of this transformation lies the revolutionary power of Artificial Intelligence (AI). In every corner of our lives, AI is making its mark, reshaping industries and redefining what we thought was possible. From healthcare to finance to entertainment, the impact of AI is undeniable. In this chapter, we will explore the profound changes brought about by AI in various sectors and delve into specific examples and case studies that illustrate its transformative power.

Let us begin with healthcare, an industry that stands to benefit immensely from the advancements in AI technology. Imagine a future where diagnoses are made with unparalleled accuracy and treatment plans are tailored specifically to each individual's needs. This reality is already taking shape with the help of AI-powered medical imaging systems that can detect diseases like cancer at an early stage, greatly improving patient outcomes. Furthermore, AI algorithms can analyze vast amounts of patient data to identify patterns and predict potential health risks before they become critical. This not only saves lives but also reduces healthcare costs by preventing unnecessary hospitalizations.

In finance, AI algorithms have revolutionized trading strategies by analyzing market trends and making split-second decisions that were once unimaginable for human traders. These systems can process colossal amounts of data in real-time, identifying patterns and anomalies that elude human perception. As a result, financial institutions have seen increased efficiency in their operations while minimizing risks associated with human error.

The entertainment industry has also been profoundly impacted by AI technologies. Streaming platforms like Netflix use sophisticated algorithms to recommend personalized content based on users' viewing history and preferences. This level of personalization enhances user experience while maximizing engagement on their platforms. Moreover, filmmakers are leveraging AI techniques for creating stunning visual effects and realistic animations previously unattainable without significant time and resources.

These examples merely scratch the surface of how AI is transforming industries across the board. However, it's important to note that the impact of AI extends beyond specific sectors; it permeates every aspect of our society. From transportation to agriculture, AI is streamlining processes, increasing productivity, and improving efficiency in ways we never thought possible.

The AI Revolution is not merely a technological shift; it's a cultural and societal one as well. With such rapid advancements come ethical considerations and questions about the future landscape of work. As AI becomes increasingly integrated into our daily lives, we must ensure that its implementation is guided by principles that prioritize human values and well-being. It is crucial to strike a balance between harnessing the power of AI while preserving human agency and dignity.

The impact of AI on various industries is profound and far-reaching. This chapter has provided an overview of how healthcare, finance, and entertainment have been revolutionized by AI technologies. From increased accuracy in medical diagnoses to personalized content recommendations, AI has transformed these sectors for the better. However, as we embrace this new era, we must also be mindful of the ethical implications and societal impacts that come with it. The future holds great promise for an increasingly AI-driven world, but only through responsible development can we ensure a future where humans coexist harmoniously with intelligent machines.

And so begins our journey into The AI Revolution - a world where possibilities are endless and innovation knows no bounds.

## Personal Stories of AI Impact

In a world where technology is advancing at an extraordinary pace, it is easy to overlook the profound impact that artificial intelligence (AI) is having on our everyday lives. From the moment we wake up to the time we go to bed, AI is silently working behind the scenes, improving our experiences and shaping our futures. In this chapter, we will delve into personal stories that highlight the positive influence of AI technologies and how they have transformed individuals' lives.

Meet Sarah, a young mother who was once burdened with worry when her daughter developed a mysterious illness. Doctors struggled to diagnose her condition accurately until AI algorithms analyzed vast amounts of medical data and identified a rare genetic disorder. Armed with this newfound knowledge, Sarah's daughter received targeted treatments that significantly improved her quality of life. Sarah now advocates for the integration of AI in healthcare systems, recognizing its potential to save countless lives.

But it's not just in healthcare where these technological marvels are making an impact. David, an aspiring entrepreneur in the finance industry, found himself struggling to manage his growing business effectively. With limited resources and overwhelming demands on his time, he turned to AI-powered automation tools that streamlined his operations and enhanced decision-making processes. The result? David's business flourished as he leveraged predictive analytics and machine learning algorithms to uncover hidden patterns in market trends.

Meanwhile, across town, Maria discovered a newfound passion for music thanks to personalized recommendations generated by AI algorithms. Having always been overwhelmed by the sheer volume of music available online, Maria had resigned herself to listening only to what she already knew. However, with AI-driven platforms introducing her to artists she had never heard before based on her preferences and mood analysis algorithms detecting her emotional state through facial recognition technology - Maria's world opened up like never before.

These personal stories are just glimpses into a vast landscape transformed by AI technologies; they represent the tip of an iceberg that is reshaping the way we live, work, and play. Whether it's revolutionizing healthcare, empowering entrepreneurs, or enriching our cultural experiences, AI is proving to be a catalyst for positive change in countless aspects of our lives.

As we explore these personal stories and their impact on individuals, it becomes evident that AI has the power to improve people's well-being on a grand scale. It breaks down barriers and empowers individuals to overcome challenges they once thought insurmountable. The potential of AI to transform lives is boundless, with applications ranging from personalized education platforms to autonomous vehicles that redefine transportation.

However, as we revel in the triumphs brought about by AI technologies, it is crucial not to overlook the ethical considerations embedded within this rapid transformation. Questions emerge regarding privacy rights, algorithmic bias, and job displacement. It is imperative that society navigates these complexities with caution as we strive for an inclusive future where the benefits of AI are accessible to all.

Personal stories serve as powerful testaments to the incredible impact of AI technologies on our lives. These narratives remind us of the immense potential for positive change brought about by embracing innovation and leveraging technology for good. As we embark on this journey into an increasingly AI-driven world, let us remain open-minded and curious while ensuring that ethics guide our decisions. The stories shared in this chapter are just a glimpse into what lies ahead – a future shaped by both human ingenuity and artificial intelligence working hand in hand towards progress.

And so we venture forth into uncharted territories where imagination meets reality - where machines become more than mere tools but partners in our pursuit of a better tomorrow.

## Future Trends and Expectations

The AI Revolution is upon us, and its impact on our world is only just beginning. In this chapter, we will explore the future trends and expectations that lie ahead as artificial intelligence continues to evolve. Brace yourself for a glimpse into the possibilities that await us in an increasingly AI-driven world.

As we stand at the precipice of technological advancements, it becomes crucial to consider the potential developments on the horizon. Experts predict that AI will not only continue to enhance existing technologies but also revolutionize industries yet untouched by its transformative power. From healthcare to transportation, finance to entertainment, no sector will remain untouched by the profound influence of artificial intelligence.

Ethical considerations also come into focus as AI becomes more ingrained in our daily lives. As machines make decisions previously reserved for humans, questions arise regarding accountability and responsibility. We must grapple with how to ensure fairness and transparency in algorithmic decision-making while avoiding biases or unintended consequences.

Moreover, societal impacts cannot be overlooked when envisioning a future dominated by AI. Automation has already disrupted traditional employment patterns, with entire job categories at risk of obsolescence. However, it is crucial to remember that new opportunities will emerge alongside these changes. The key lies in equipping individuals with the skills necessary for this new era and bridging any socioeconomic divides that may emerge. To gain insight into these future trends and expectations surrounding AI, we turn to research findings and expert opinions from various fields. Driven by curiosity about what awaits us, we must examine both utopian visions and dystopian fears associated with an AI-driven society.

In healthcare, imagine a world where diagnoses are made swiftly and accurately by intelligent systems analyzing vast amounts of medical data instantaneously—saving countless lives in the process. Picture self-driving cars navigating our roads seamlessly while reducing accidents caused by human error—a future where transportation becomes safer than ever before. Finance too stands poised for transformation as AI algorithms analyze market trends and make predictions with unprecedented accuracy. Investment decisions could be optimized, potentially creating new opportunities for wealth generation and economic growth.

As we venture deeper into this new frontier, it is essential to consider the potential pitfalls. Safeguarding personal privacy becomes paramount as AI systems collect and process vast amounts of data. Striking the delicate balance between convenience and security will shape our digital landscape in the years to come.

In contemplating these future trends, it is clear that the AI Revolution will continue to shape our lives in ways we cannot fully comprehend. It is a revolution fueled by innovation and curiosity, one that demands our attention and participation. The future lies before us, filled with both excitement and uncertainty. Will we embrace these advancements wholeheartedly or cautiously navigate uncharted territory? The choice lies within each of us as we embark on this journey towards an AI-driven world.

As this chapter draws to a close, let us reflect on the possibilities that await us—an era where machines collaborate with humans to achieve extraordinary feats. The AI Revolution beckons us forward into a future where boundaries are pushed, limitations shattered, and new possibilities emerge at every turn.

Are you ready? The adventure awaits!

# Chapter Two

# Demystifying AI: A Layman's Terms Approach

In the ever-evolving world of technology, few topics have captured our collective imagination quite like artificial intelligence (AI). It is a concept that seems simultaneously awe-inspiring and intimidating, often shrouded in complex terminology and unfamiliar jargon. However, understanding AI doesn't have to be an insurmountable task. In this chapter, we will embark on a journey to demystify AI by using relatable everyday analogies.

Imagine yourself behind the wheel of a car, cruising down the open road. Just as you make decisions based on your surroundings – such as slowing down when approaching a traffic light or changing lanes when necessary – AI systems also make decisions based on their environment. By drawing parallels between driving a car and how AI algorithms perceive and process information, we can begin to comprehend the underlying principles of this remarkable field.

Another analogy that can help us grasp the complexities of AI is organizing a library. Just like how librarians categorize books based on their content and assign them to specific shelves for easy access, AI algorithms use similar techniques to organize vast amounts of data efficiently. By relating this familiar experience to how AI systems sort through immense datasets and extract meaningful patterns, we can gain insight into the power and potential of these intelligent machines.

Analogies serve as invaluable tools in simplifying abstract concepts by linking them to familiar experiences. Picture yourself cooking a meal following a recipe – you carefully measure ingredients, follow step-by-step instructions, adjust seasoning to taste, all while having an overall goal in mind: creating a delicious dish. Similarly, AI models "learn" from vast amounts of training data and algorithms designed to optimize specific tasks or objectives.

Let's consider one more analogy before we delve deeper into understanding the fundamental principles behind AI. Imagine playing chess against an opponent who always seems one step ahead – making moves that anticipate your every move. This strategic brilliance is akin to AI's ability to analyze countless possibilities and make calculated decisions in real-time, allowing machines to outperform humans in complex tasks.

By employing these everyday analogies, we can navigate the intricacies of AI with greater ease. Understanding the underlying principles and applications becomes less daunting when we relate them to experiences that are already familiar to us. Just as a car navigates the roads, a library organizes knowledge, cooking follows recipes, and chess requires strategic thinking – so too does AI rely on algorithms, data processing, and decision-making.

Throughout this book, we will explore various other analogies that shed light on different aspects of AI. We will discover how interactive learning exercises can further enhance our understanding by providing hands-on opportunities to experiment with AI principles. Additionally, we will explore the use of visual aids such as infographics and diagrams as powerful tools for simplifying abstract ideas related to AI.

The journey ahead promises not only a demystification of AI but also an exploration of its ethical implications and future possibilities. We will delve into practical implementation strategies while addressing common challenges faced when working with AI systems. By the end of this book, you'll be equipped with a comprehensive understanding of the world of AI – from its fundamental concepts to its potential impact on society.

So buckle up and get ready for an exhilarating ride through Demystifying AI: A Layman's Terms Approach! Together, we'll unravel the mysteries behind this groundbreaking technology one analogy at a time.

**Interactive Learning Exercises**

As we delve deeper into the realm of artificial intelligence, it is crucial to actively engage with the fundamental principles that underpin this fascinating field. In this chapter, we will embark on a journey of interactive learning exercises that will allow you, the reader, to not only comprehend but also apply basic AI principles in a hands-on manner. By actively participating in these exercises, you will not only solidify your knowledge but also gain practical insights into the world of AI. Imagine yourself as an explorer venturing into uncharted territory. As you take your first steps into this new domain, think of these interactive exercises as your map and compass, guiding you through unfamiliar terrain and illuminating the path ahead.

In our first exercise, let's imagine that you are a robotic car navigating through a busy city street. Your task is to understand how artificial intelligence algorithms can enable a car to make autonomous decisions on the road while ensuring safety for both passengers and pedestrians. Through simulation software or even physical models like remote-controlled cars equipped with AI capabilities, you can experience firsthand how machine learning algorithms analyze real-time data from sensors such as cameras and lidar to make split-second decisions on acceleration, braking, and steering.

By actively engaging with this exercise, you will grasp the intricate relationship between input data and intelligent decision-making. You will witness how algorithms learn from patterns in data and continuously adapt their behavior based on feedback received from their environment. Moving forward in our exploration of AI applications through interactive exercises, let us now delve into natural language processing (NLP). Imagine yourself as an AI-powered virtual assistant like Siri or Alexa. Your mission is to understand spoken commands from users and respond appropriately using natural language understanding techniques.

Through speech recognition software or text-to-speech applications integrated with NLP capabilities, you can engage in conversations with these virtual assistants. Experiment with different commands and observe how they interpret your words using algorithms trained on vast amounts of language data. This exercise will provide you with a firsthand experience of how AI systems can comprehend and respond to human language, opening doors to a world where machines understand and interact with us in a more human-like manner.

As our exploration continues, we now turn our attention to computer vision and image recognition. Imagine yourself as an AI-powered image classifier. Your task is to analyze images and identify objects within them accurately.

Through interactive platforms or even simple online quizzes, you can test your skills in recognizing objects from various images. By experimenting with different algorithms and training models on labeled datasets, you will develop an understanding of how AI systems can interpret visual information, distinguish between different objects, and classify them accordingly. This exercise will unveil the power of AI in unlocking insights from visual data – a skill that has transformative applications across industries such as healthcare, security, and entertainment.

As we conclude this chapter on interactive learning exercises, let us reflect on the invaluable experiences these hands-on activities offer. By actively engaging with AI principles through simulated scenarios or interactive platforms, you gain practical insights into the inner workings of this remarkable field. These exercises not only deepen your understanding but also empower you to apply your knowledge in real-world contexts.

So embrace these interactive learning exercises as stepping stones towards mastering the complexities of artificial intelligence. Let them be your gateway to unlocking the immense potential that lies within this ever-evolving field. Remember that the more actively you participate, the greater your understanding of AI's applications and potential becomes.

Now venture forth into these interactive experiences with curiosity and enthusiasm! The realm of artificial intelligence awaits your exploration like an uncharted territory full of endless possibilities.

**Visual Learning Aids**

As we delve deeper into the world of artificial intelligence (AI), it becomes evident that understanding its abstract concepts can be quite challenging. The complexities of AI can often leave us feeling overwhelmed and disconnected from its true potential. However, fear not, for in this chapter, we will explore the power of visual learning aids in demystifying AI and making it more accessible to everyone.

Imagine you are embarking on a journey to a foreign land, where you don't speak the language. You arrive at the airport, and instead of being greeted by signs in a language you can understand, you are faced with a sea of incomprehensible symbols and characters. It is disorienting and frustrating. But then, someone hands you a map - a visual representation that guides your way through unfamiliar territory. Suddenly, everything becomes clearer and more manageable.

Similarly, in our quest to understand AI concepts, visual learning aids serve as our maps through uncharted intellectual terrain. Infographics and diagrams provide us with clear visuals and intuitive illustrations that simplify complex ideas related to AI. They allow us to see how different components work together harmoniously, like pieces fitting into a grand puzzle.

Picture this: You want to explain machine learning algorithms to someone who has no prior knowledge of AI. You could start by describing how these algorithms analyze vast amounts of data to identify patterns or make predictions – but words alone might not suffice in capturing the essence of their functionality. Instead, imagine showing them an infographic where data flows through interconnected nodes like rivers converging into an ocean of knowledge. This visual representation brings clarity by illustrating how machine learning algorithms learn from data inputs and generate insights.

Visual learning aids also help us grasp abstract concepts by providing tangible connections between real-world experiences and AI principles. Let's say you want to explain natural language processing (NLP) – the branch of AI that enables machines to understand human language – to someone unfamiliar with the intricacies of AI. You could start by comparing NLP to a skilled translator who can effortlessly convert words from one language into another. By using this analogy, you bridge the gap between their existing knowledge and the new concept, making it easier for them to understand how NLP works.

Furthermore, visual learning aids offer us a holistic view of AI systems, showcasing how different components interact and influence one another. Just like an orchestra, where each instrument plays its part in creating a harmonious symphony, AI systems consist of various elements that work together to achieve their intended goals. With the help of diagrams and flowcharts, we can visualize these interactions and gain a deeper understanding of the underlying mechanisms driving AI technology.

Now that we have explored the power of visual learning aids in demystifying AI, it is important to emphasize their role in making this daunting field more accessible and comprehensible for everyone. By providing clear visuals and intuitive illustrations, infographics and diagrams break down complex concepts into digestible pieces. They enable us to see beyond abstract theories and truly grasp the inner workings of AI.

As we journey through this book on demystifying AI in layman's terms, let us embrace these visual learning aids as our companions on this enlightening adventure. Together with everyday analogies, interactive exercises, ethical considerations, future possibilities, practical implementation guidance, and strategies for overcoming challenges – all chapters yet to be explored – they will equip us with the necessary tools to navigate the vast landscape of artificial intelligence.

So let us now embark on our exploration through visual realms as we unveil the secrets behind artificial intelligence's intricate tapestry - one vivid illustration at a time.

**Ethical Implications**

In a world driven by technology, the rise of artificial intelligence (AI) brings about numerous ethical considerations that demand our examination. As AI systems become more integrated into various domains such as healthcare, finance, and surveillance, it is crucial to explore the ethical implications that accompany their deployment. From bias in algorithms to privacy concerns and potential job displacement, this chapter seeks to shed light on both the benefits and risks associated with AI technologies.

When we think of AI, we often envision unbiased decision-making based purely on data. However, algorithms can inadvertently perpetuate biases present in the data they are trained on. For instance, if historical data includes racial or gender biases, these biases can be amplified by an algorithm without proper checks and balances. This raises important questions about fairness and equality in decision-making processes powered by AI. Addressing this issue requires careful consideration and evaluation of training data to ensure that algorithms do not perpetuate or reinforce existing biases.

Another ethical concern surrounding AI lies in the realm of privacy. With vast amounts of personal information being collected for analysis by AI systems, there is a need for robust safeguards to protect individuals' privacy rights. Striking a balance between utilizing data for meaningful insights and respecting individuals' right to privacy is essential in building trust with users. Transparent communication regarding data collection practices and clear consent mechanisms are vital steps towards safeguarding privacy in an increasingly connected world.

Furthermore, as AI continues to advance, there is growing concern about potential job displacement caused by automation. While some argue that AI will create new job opportunities that require human creativity and problem-solving skills, others fear widespread unemployment due to machines replacing human labor. It is crucial for society to anticipate these shifts and proactively invest in retraining programs and education initiatives that equip individuals with skills needed for emerging roles in an AI-driven world.

To illustrate these ethical considerations in practice, let's examine healthcare as an example domain. AI has the potential to revolutionize healthcare by improving diagnosis accuracy, optimizing treatment plans, and enhancing patient care. However, implementing AI in healthcare also raises ethical dilemmas. For instance, how do we ensure that AI algorithms are unbiased and do not disproportionately impact marginalized communities? How do we balance the benefits of data-driven decision-making with patient autonomy and informed consent? These questions require careful reflection and collaboration between technologists, ethicists, policymakers, and healthcare professionals.

While the ethical implications of AI may seem daunting at first glance, it is crucial to approach them with an open mind and a commitment to responsible development and deployment. Striving for transparency in algorithmic decision-making processes, promoting diversity in AI development teams, and engaging in public discourse are all steps towards addressing these ethical concerns.

As we navigate the intricate landscape of AI ethics, it is essential to strike a balance between harnessing the transformative power of AI while safeguarding fundamental human values. By acknowledging these ethical considerations head-on, we can shape a future where AI technologies are utilized responsibly for the betterment of society.

# Chapter Three

# From Turing to Today: A Historical Journey

**U**nveiling the Marvels of Narrow AI

In this captivating chapter, we delve into the extraordinary world of narrow AI, where machines possess the ability to perform specific tasks with astonishing precision and finesse. Prepare to be astounded as we traverse through a myriad of practical examples, from virtual personal assistants that seem to read our minds to recommendation systems that anticipate our every desire. As we embark on this enlightening journey, it is crucial to understand the essence of narrow AI. Unlike its more complex counterpart, general AI, which possesses human-like cognitive abilities across various domains, narrow AI hones in on excelling at particular tasks within a limited scope. It is the epitome of specialization and proficiency.

Picture this: you wake up in the morning, groggy and disheveled from a restless night's sleep. You stumble into your kitchen, feeling overwhelmed by the endless possibilities for breakfast. But fear not! With just a few words uttered to your trusty virtual personal assistant - an embodiment of narrow AI - you are swiftly guided towards culinary perfection. This remarkable companion analyzes your preferences with such deftness that it feels like magic unfolding before your eyes.

Virtual personal assistants have revolutionized our daily lives with their uncanny ability to comprehend natural language and seamlessly interact with us as if they were another sentient being. Whether it's Siri or Alexa responding at lightning speed or Google Assistant delivering spot-on answers to our burning inquiries, these digital marvels embody the power of narrow AI in its purest form.

But wait! There's more! As we progress further into this chapter brimming with wonderment, we encounter recommendation systems that are nothing short of prodigious. These intelligent algorithms have mastered the art of anticipation by meticulously studying our preferences and patterns. Imagine browsing through an online store searching for that perfect outfit for an upcoming event. Suddenly, like a serendipitous stroke from fate itself, you find yourself immersed in a world of tailored suggestions, each item handpicked just for you. This is the work of recommendation systems, an awe-inspiring manifestation of narrow AI at its finest.

These ingenious systems meticulously analyze vast amounts of data, scrutinizing your past purchases, browsing history, and even the preferences of others with similar tastes. In a symphony of algorithms and computations, they orchestrate a harmonious blend of convenience and personalization. While the applications we have explored thus far are undeniably remarkable, it is important to note that narrow AI extends far beyond our personal lives. Industries such as healthcare, finance, and transportation have embraced this technological marvel with open arms. From diagnosing diseases with unparalleled accuracy to optimizing financial portfolios based on market trends, narrow AI has become an indispensable ally in our quest for progress.

Dear reader, we have traversed through the captivating realm of narrow AI, where machines possess an uncanny ability to excel at specific tasks that leave us in awe. From virtual personal assistants that seem sentient to recommendation systems that anticipate our desires effortlessly - these practical examples showcase the true potential of narrow AI.

**The Uncharted Path to General Intelligence**

In the vast realm of artificial intelligence, there exists a quest that consumes the minds of brilliant innovators and pioneers. It is the pursuit of achieving what is known as general intelligence—a concept so grand, so elusive, that it transcends mere algorithms and enters the realm of true cognition. As we delve into this chapter, dear readers, be prepared to embark on a journey like no other—one that will unravel the challenges and ongoing research in developing general or superintelligent AI.

To comprehend the magnitude of this endeavor, we must first grasp the essence of general intelligence itself. Unlike narrow AI systems designed for specific tasks, such as playing chess or recognizing images, general intelligence aims to replicate human-like cognitive abilities across a broad range of domains. Picture an AI system capable of reasoning, learning from experience, and adapting to novel situations—truly an awe-inspiring prospect.

However, dear readers, tread carefully upon this path strewn with obstacles. For within lies the crux of our quest—the hurdles that impede our progress towards achieving such profound machine cognition. One such challenge arises from understanding how human brains function at a fundamental level. While neuroscience offers tantalizing glimpses into our neural networks' intricacies, deciphering their complexity remains an enigma yet to be fully unraveled.

Another hurdle nestled within this labyrinthine journey concerns knowledge representation—a crucial facet for any intelligent entity. Humans possess an innate ability to absorb information from varied sources and seamlessly link ideas together—a skill we often take for granted. Yet replicating this amalgamation of knowledge in machines proves no easy feat; it requires devising novel methods for efficient data representation and retrieval.

Furthermore, dear readers, envision a world where AI systems can autonomously learn from their experiences—the hallmark of true cognition. Alas! In reality's cruel embrace lies yet another obstacle—the formidable challenge posed by lifelong learning. Unlike traditional machine learning paradigms, which rely on fixed datasets, achieving lifelong learning necessitates the capacity to continually adapt and evolve in response to new information. A task that demands a delicate balance between stability and plasticity—a conundrum that continues to perplex AI researchers.

Nonetheless, dear readers, fret not. The pursuit of general intelligence marches onward, fueled by the relentless dedication of brilliant minds worldwide. Amidst these challenges lie the beacons of hope—the ongoing research endeavors that illuminate our path towards this audacious ambition.

One such avenue lies in the realm of deep reinforcement learning—a paradigm that combines the power of artificial neural networks with the principles of reward-based learning. By imbuing AI systems with the ability to learn from trial and error, researchers strive to bridge the gap between narrow AI and general intelligence. Through iterative interactions with environments rich in complexity, these nascent algorithms inch closer to understanding nuanced decision-making—a feat once reserved solely for human minds.

Moreover, dear readers, imagine a future where machines can grasp abstract concepts as effortlessly as we do—where they possess an innate understanding of language's intricate nuances. Enter natural language processing (NLP), an ever-evolving field seeking to imbue machines with linguistic prowess. By unraveling language's intricate tapestry through advanced techniques like deep learning and semantic analysis, NLP takes us one step closer towards realizing our grand vision.

As this chapter draws to a close, my fellow enthusiasts in AI exploration, let us revel in our shared passion for unlocking the mysteries held within general intelligence's embrace. Though obstacles may loom large on this path less traveled by human intellects alone—through perseverance and unwavering determination—we shall surmount them all. And so it is here we part ways for now—knowing that beyond these pages lie countless discoveries yet untold; secrets yearning to be unearthed by those who dare challenge convention and embrace possibility itself.

### The Profound Impact of AI

In the vast expanse of our ever-evolving society, where human ingenuity and technological prowess intertwine, a revolution is underway. It is a revolution fueled by the remarkable capabilities of Artificial Intelligence (AI). As we delve deeper into this chapter, we shall embark upon a journey to unravel the profound impact that different types of AI have on various aspects of our society.

With each passing day, AI becomes an omnipresent force in our lives, leaving no stone unturned as it permeates industries and sectors far and wide. From the bustling realms of job markets to the delicate landscape of healthcare, the transformative power of AI knows no bounds. As we venture forth into this chapter's exploration, let us peel back the layers and discover how this extraordinary technology shapes our world.

The first type of AI that demands our attention is Machine Learning (ML), a marvel that empowers computers to learn from data without explicit programming. ML algorithms analyze vast troves of information with unparalleled speed and precision, unraveling patterns and insights invisible to human eyes. This technological wizardry has ignited a seismic shift in industries like finance, where algorithms can now predict market trends with astonishing accuracy.

Imagine stepping into a world where medical diagnoses are enhanced by AI's discerning eye – an era where doctors are armed with powerful tools capable of detecting diseases at their incipient stages. This brings us to another impactful type of AI known as Predictive Analytics. By analyzing immense volumes of patient data, intelligent systems can predict health risks before symptoms even manifest themselves – an invaluable breakthrough in disease prevention.

As we traverse further down this captivating path, Natural Language Processing (NLP) emerges as yet another luminous star in the constellation of artificial intelligence types. NLP enables machines to comprehend human language - deciphering its subtleties and nuances like never before. From virtual assistants interpreting voice commands to language translation apps bridging cultural divides, NLP has revolutionized the way we interact with technology.

Now, let us turn our gaze towards the profound influence of AI on the job market. Automation and robotics have long been synonymous with fear and anxiety for workers around the globe. However, it is crucial to acknowledge that while certain job roles may be rendered obsolete, AI also brings forth an abundance of new opportunities. By automating routine tasks, AI frees human potential to embrace creativity and innovation – fostering a future where work becomes more fulfilling and meaningful.

In this brave new world driven by AI's omnipresence, we must also grapple with ethical considerations. As intelligent systems make decisions once reserved solely for humans, questions arise regarding accountability and transparency. It is imperative that we establish frameworks to ensure fairness and avoid biases ingrained within algorithms - safeguarding against unintended consequences that could otherwise emerge from unchecked technological advancement.

As our journey through this chapter draws to a close, let us reflect upon the transformative power of AI types on society. We stand at the precipice of an era where machines augment human capabilities rather than replace them – where boundaries are shattered and possibilities multiplied. Embrace this technological revolution with open arms, for it holds the key to a brighter future where human potential knows no limits.

# Types of AI: Narrow to General Intelligence

**U**nveiling the Marvels of Narrow AI

In this captivating chapter, we delve into the extraordinary world of narrow AI, where machines possess the ability to perform specific tasks with astonishing precision and finesse. Prepare to be astounded as we traverse through a myriad of practical examples, from virtual personal assistants that seem to read our minds to recommendation systems that anticipate our every desire. As we embark on this enlightening journey, it is crucial to understand the essence of narrow AI. Unlike its more complex counterpart, general AI, which possesses human-like cognitive abilities across various domains, narrow

AI hones in on excelling at particular tasks within a limited scope. It is the epitome of specialization and proficiency.

Picture this: you wake up in the morning, groggy and disheveled from a restless night's sleep. You stumble into your kitchen, feeling overwhelmed by the endless possibilities for breakfast. But fear not! With just a few words uttered to your trusty virtual personal assistant - an embodiment of narrow AI - you are swiftly guided towards culinary perfection. This remarkable companion analyzes your preferences with such deftness that it feels like magic unfolding before your eyes.

Virtual personal assistants have revolutionized our daily lives with their uncanny ability to comprehend natural language and seamlessly interact with us as if they were another sentient being. Whether it's Siri or Alexa responding at lightning speed or Google Assistant delivering spot-on answers to our burning inquiries, these digital marvels embody the power of narrow AI in its purest form.

But wait! There's more! As we progress further into this chapter brimming with wonderment, we encounter recommendation systems that are nothing short of prodigious. These intelligent algorithms have mastered the art of anticipation by meticulously studying our preferences and patterns.

Imagine browsing through an online store searching for that perfect outfit for an upcoming event. Suddenly, like a serendipitous stroke from fate itself, you find yourself immersed in a world of tailored suggestions, each item handpicked just for you. This is the work of recommendation systems, an awe-inspiring manifestation of narrow

AI at its finest. These ingenious systems meticulously analyze vast amounts of data, scrutinizing your past purchases, browsing history, and even the preferences of others with similar tastes. In a symphony of algorithms and computations, they orchestrate a harmonious blend of convenience and personalization.

While the applications we have explored thus far are undeniably remarkable, it is important to note that narrow AI extends far beyond our personal lives. Industries such as healthcare, finance, and transportation have embraced this technological marvel with open arms. From diagnosing diseases with unparalleled accuracy to optimizing financial portfolios based on market trends, narrow AI has become an indispensable ally in our quest for progress.

Dear reader, we have traversed through the captivating realm of narrow AI, where machines possess an uncanny ability to excel at specific tasks that leave us in awe. From virtual personal assistants that seem sentient to recommendation systems that anticipate our desires effortlessly - these practical examples showcase the true potential of narrow AI. Remember that behind every seemingly magical feat lies intricate algorithms and meticulous analysis. The future holds endless possibilities as we continue to unravel the mysteries hidden within this cutting-edge technology. So brace yourself for what lies ahead because extraordinary wonders await us on this exhilarating journey into understanding AI.

## The Uncharted Path to General Intelligence

In the vast realm of artificial intelligence, there exists a quest that consumes the minds of brilliant innovators and pioneers. It is the pursuit of achieving what is known as general intelligence—a concept so grand, so elusive, that it transcends mere algorithms and enters the realm of true cognition. As we delve into this chapter, dear readers, be prepared to embark on a journey like no other—one that will unravel the challenges and ongoing research in developing general or superintelligent AI.

To comprehend the magnitude of this endeavor, we must first grasp the essence of general intelligence itself. Unlike narrow AI systems designed for specific tasks, such as playing chess or recognizing images, general intelligence aims to replicate human-like cognitive abilities across a broad range of domains. Picture an AI system capable of reasoning, learning from experience, and adapting to novel situations—truly an awe-inspiring prospect.

However, dear readers, tread carefully upon this path strewn with obstacles. For within lies the crux of our quest—the hurdles that impede our progress towards achieving such profound machine cognition. One such challenge arises from understanding how human brains function at a fundamental level. While neuroscience offers tantalizing glimpses into our neural networks' intricacies, deciphering their complexity remains an enigma yet to be fully unraveled.

Another hurdle nestled within this labyrinthine journey concerns knowledge representation—a crucial facet for any intelligent entity. Humans possess an innate ability to absorb information from varied sources and seamlessly link ideas together—a skill we often take for granted. Yet replicating this amalgamation of knowledge in machines proves no easy feat; it requires devising novel methods for efficient data representation and retrieval.

Furthermore, dear readers, envision a world where AI systems can autonomously learn from their experiences—the hallmark of true cognition. Alas! In reality's cruel embrace lies yet another obstacle—the formidable challenge posed by lifelong learning. Unlike traditional machine learning paradigms, which rely on fixed datasets, achieving lifelong learning necessitates the capacity to continually adapt and evolve in response to new information. A task that demands a delicate balance between stability and plasticity—a conundrum that continues to perplex AI researchers. Nonetheless, dear readers, fret not. The pursuit of general intelligence marches onward, fueled by the relentless dedication of brilliant minds worldwide. Amidst these challenges lie the beacons of hope—the ongoing research endeavors that illuminate our path towards this audacious ambition.

One such avenue lies in the realm of deep reinforcement learning—a paradigm that combines the power of artificial neural networks with the principles of reward-based learning. By imbuing AI systems with the ability to learn from trial and error, researchers strive to bridge the gap between narrow AI and general intelligence. Through iterative interactions with environments rich in complexity, these nascent algorithms inch closer to understanding nuanced decision-making—a feat once reserved solely for human minds.

Moreover, dear readers, imagine a future where machines can grasp abstract concepts as effortlessly as we do—where they possess an innate understanding of language's intricate nuances. Enter natural language processing (NLP), an ever-evolving field seeking to imbue machines with linguistic prowess. By unraveling language's intricate tapestry through advanced techniques like deep learning and semantic analysis, NLP takes us one step closer towards realizing our grand vision.

Let us revel in our shared passion for unlocking the mysteries held within general intelligence's embrace. Though obstacles may loom large on this path less traveled by human intellects alone—through perseverance and unwavering determination—we shall surmount them all. And so it is here we part ways for now—knowing that beyond these pages lie countless discoveries yet untold; secrets yearning to be unearthed by those who dare challenge convention and embrace possibility itself.

## Revolutionizing Society - The Profound Impact of AI

In the vast expanse of our ever-evolving society, where human ingenuity and technological prowess intertwine, a revolution is underway. It is a revolution fueled by the remarkable capabilities of Artificial Intelligence (AI). As we delve deeper into this chapter, we shall embark upon a journey to unravel the profound impact that different types of AI have on various aspects of our society.

With each passing day, AI becomes an omnipresent force in our lives, leaving no stone unturned as it permeates industries and sectors far and wide. From the bustling realms of job markets to the delicate landscape of healthcare, the transformative power of AI knows no bounds. As we venture forth into this chapter's exploration, let us peel back the layers and discover how this extraordinary technology shapes our world.

The first type of AI that demands our attention is Machine Learning (ML), a marvel that empowers computers to learn from data without explicit programming. ML algorithms analyze vast troves of information with unparalleled speed and precision, unraveling patterns and insights invisible to human eyes. This technological wizardry has ignited a seismic shift in industries like finance, where algorithms can now predict market trends with astonishing accuracy.

Imagine stepping into a world where medical diagnoses are enhanced by AI's discerning eye – an era where doctors are armed with powerful tools capable of detecting diseases at their incipient stages. This brings us to another impactful type of AI known as Predictive Analytics. By analyzing immense volumes of patient data, intelligent systems can predict health risks before symptoms even manifest themselves – an invaluable breakthrough in disease prevention.

As we traverse further down this captivating path, Natural Language Processing (NLP) emerges as yet another luminous star in the constellation of artificial intelligence types. NLP enables machines to comprehend human language - deciphering its subtleties and nuances like never before. From virtual assistants interpreting voice commands to language translation apps bridging cultural divides, NLP has revolutionized the way we interact with technology.

Now, let us turn our gaze towards the profound influence of AI on the job market. Automation and robotics have long been synonymous with fear and anxiety for workers around the globe. However, it is crucial to acknowledge that while certain job roles may be rendered obsolete, AI also brings forth an abundance of new opportunities. By automating routine tasks, AI frees human potential to embrace creativity and innovation – fostering a future where work becomes more fulfilling and meaningful.

In this brave new world driven by AI's omnipresence, we must also grapple with ethical considerations. As intelligent systems make decisions once reserved solely for humans, questions arise regarding accountability and transparency. It is imperative that we establish frameworks to ensure fairness and avoid biases ingrained within algorithms - safeguarding against unintended consequences that could otherwise emerge from unchecked technological advancement.

As our journey through this chapter draws to a close, let us reflect upon the transformative power of AI types on society. We stand at the precipice of an era where machines augment human capabilities rather than replace them – where boundaries are shattered and possibilities multiplied. Embrace this technological revolution with open arms, for it holds the key to a brighter future where human potential knows no limits.

# Chapter Five

# Machine Learning Unveiled

**U**nveiling the Mysteries of Supervised Learning

In the vast realm of artificial intelligence, where innovation and discovery intertwine, there exists a fascinating concept known as supervised learning. Brace yourself, dear reader, for an enchanting journey into the depths of this captivating field. In this chapter, we shall unravel the intricacies of supervised learning and explore its remarkable applications in real-world scenarios. At its core, supervised learning is akin to a nurturing mentor guiding a fledgling apprentice towards mastery. Picture a wise sage imparting wisdom and knowledge to an eager student; such is the essence of this remarkable form of machine learning. As we delve deeper into this chapter, prepare to be captivated by tales of algorithms that learn from labeled data and make predictions with astonishing accuracy.

The fundamental principle behind supervised learning lies in its reliance on labeled datasets. These datasets act as beacons illuminating the path towards enlightenment. Just as an artist harnesses their palette to create artistry, so too do these labeled datasets provide the foundation upon which models are trained.

Imagine wandering through a verdant forest where each tree represents a data point with corresponding labels. The model's purpose is to discern patterns amidst this lush tapestry and use these patterns to predict future outcomes accurately. This process mirrors how humans learn from experiences and observations — it's truly awe-inspiring. Now that we have laid down the groundwork for understanding supervised learning let us embark on an expedition through its practical applications in various domains.

In our first stop on this extraordinary journey, we find ourselves immersed in the realm of healthcare. Picture doctors equipped with cutting-edge technology that aids them in diagnosing diseases swiftly and accurately. Through supervised learning algorithms trained on vast medical databases containing patient records coupled with diagnoses, these models can analyze symptoms and predict possible afflictions with astounding precision.

Next on our itinerary takes us deep into the heartland of finance—a world brimming with numbers, risk, and uncertainty. Here, supervised learning lends its prowess to predict stock market fluctuations, enabling investors to make informed decisions amidst the turbulence of financial markets. With the aid of labeled historical data encompassing market trends and economic indicators, these algorithms can forecast price movements with astonishing accuracy.

As we journey further into the realm of supervised learning, we encounter an enchanting landscape inhabited by autonomous vehicles. These cutting-edge marvels rely on vast datasets collected from sensors and cameras to navigate roads safely and efficiently. Through meticulous training using labeled data showcasing various traffic scenarios, these models become adept at making real-time decisions that mirror human intuition.

Our expedition through the realms of supervised learning draws to a close; however, the knowledge gained shall linger forever in our minds like cherished memories from a grand adventure. We have witnessed how this remarkable field imparts intelligence upon machines through labeled datasets and empowers them to make predictions that rival human capabilities.

**Unveiling the Mysteries of Unsupervised Learning**

In the vast realm of artificial intelligence, where machines are granted the power to learn and adapt, unsupervised learning stands as a beacon of untapped potential. Welcome, dear reader, to another captivating chapter of "Understanding AI: A Comprehensive Guide for Beginners." Today, we embark on an enthralling journey through the fascinating world of unsupervised learning applications. Brace yourself for an exploration that will shed light on the enigmatic tasks of clustering and pattern recognition.

Like a skilled detective unearthing hidden connections in a complex web of data, unsupervised learning algorithms possess remarkable abilities. They have the uncanny aptitude to uncover patterns and structures without needing predefined labels or guidance from human experts. This extraordinary capacity makes them invaluable in various domains where uncovering hidden insights is paramount.

Imagine traversing vast fields teeming with flowers yet lacking any discernible organization. As you venture forth with curiosity fueling your every step, you stumble upon a revelation: these flowers have distinct characteristics that allow them to be grouped into clusters based on colors, shapes, or sizes. Such is the power bestowed upon us by unsupervised learning algorithms - they enable us to decipher intricate patterns and bring order to apparent chaos.

Clustering serves as one of the principal applications within unsupervised learning paradigms. It allows us to group similar objects together based on shared attributes or features. Picture yourself navigating through a dense forest filled with countless species of trees - some bearing broad leaves while others boast slender trunks that stretch towards the heavens. By employing clustering techniques rooted in unsupervised learning algorithms, we can unravel nature's secrets and identify distinct groups among these arboreal wonders.

The significance of clustering extends far beyond botany; it permeates numerous domains such as customer segmentation in marketing or anomaly detection in cybersecurity. Within commerce's bustling landscape lies an insatiable desire to comprehend consumer behavior and preferences. Through unsupervised learning, we can unravel intricate patterns, grouping customers into clusters based on their buying habits or demographic attributes. This enables businesses to tailor their products and services with unparalleled precision, captivating the hearts and minds of their target audience.

Pattern recognition flourishes as yet another captivating application within the realm of unsupervised learning. In a world awash with information, our minds yearn for methods to distill meaning from chaos; this is where pattern recognition unveils its true brilliance. Imagine gazing at an abstract painting - an amalgamation of vibrant brushstrokes that seem devoid of order or structure. Yet, within this artistic ensemble lies a symphony of hidden patterns waiting to be discovered.

Through the omniscient lens of unsupervised learning algorithms, we can unlock these concealed patterns in a multitude of domains. From medical diagnostics to fraud detection systems, pattern recognition empowers us to identify anomalies or abnormalities by discerning recurring motifs within vast datasets. As we delve deeper into this chapter's labyrinthine corridors, you will witness firsthand how unsupervised learning unravels mysteries that would otherwise remain concealed beneath layers of complexity.

As our expedition through the boundless realm of unsupervised learning applications draws near its conclusion, we find ourselves standing at the precipice between knowledge and wonderment. The power held by these algorithms transcends mere data processing; they possess the ability to illuminate hidden connections and uncover truths that lay dormant within massive datasets.

**The Power of Reinforcement Learning Unleashed**

In the vast realm of artificial intelligence, where algorithms dance with data and machines mimic human cognition, one particular technique stands tall as a beacon of innovation and ingenuity: reinforcement learning. Brace yourself, dear reader, for we are about to embark on a thrilling journey that will illuminate how this remarkable method permeates the realms of gaming, robotics, and decision-making processes.

Imagine a virtual world where players are transported to uncharted territories and tasked with conquering formidable challenges. This is the domain where reinforcement learning flexes its mighty muscles, transforming ordinary gaming experiences into extraordinary adventures. With each interaction between player and game environment, an intelligent agent learns from its actions through a process of trial and error. By receiving feedback in the form of rewards or penalties based on its decisions, the agent evolves over time to make better choices and achieve ultimate success.

But wait! It doesn't stop there. Reinforcement learning's impact extends far beyond the boundaries of virtual reality. In the realm of robotics, intelligent machines are mastering tasks that were once deemed solely human endeavors. Picture a robot delicately assembling intricate components with unparalleled precision or navigating treacherous terrain with unwavering grace. These feats are made possible by imbuing robots with reinforcement learning algorithms.

By combining sensory perception with an insatiable hunger for knowledge, robots learn from their environment just like we humans do—through experience. They adapt their behaviors based on rewards or punishments received during their interactions with the world around them. Through countless iterations and fine-tuning of their algorithms, these mechanical marvels become adept at manipulating objects, grasping complex concepts, and even collaborating seamlessly alongside their human counterparts.

Beyond gaming and robotics lies another profound application for reinforcement learning—decision-making processes that shape our daily lives in ways both big and small. Whether it's determining optimal routes for transportation systems or optimizing energy consumption in smart grids, this technique revolutionizes the way we make choices and maximize outcomes.

Consider the intricacies of stock market trading, where every decision carries the weight of potential fortunes gained or lost. Reinforcement learning algorithms analyze vast amounts of historical data, detecting patterns and predicting future trends. With each trade executed, these algorithms learn from their successes and failures, continuously adapting their strategies to optimize returns.

In the midst of this technological revolution, it is imperative to acknowledge the challenges that accompany such power. Ethical considerations must be at the forefront as we navigate uncharted territories. As reinforcement learning evolves, questions arise regarding accountability and transparency in decision-making processes. Striking a delicate balance between innovation and responsibility becomes paramount to ensure a harmonious coexistence between humans and machines.

Dear reader, as we bid farewell to this enthralling chapter on reinforcement learning's triumphant foray into gaming, robotics, and decision-making processes, let us marvel at its boundless potential. From virtual worlds that transport us to realms yet undiscovered to robots that seamlessly integrate into our daily lives with awe-inspiring finesse—we are witnessing AI's ascent towards greatness. Revel in wonder as you envision a future where machines become our loyal companions—guiding us through treacherous quests in virtual realities or lending a helping hand in navigating life's labyrinthine paths. The power of reinforcement learning has been unleashed—forever altering the course of human history with its insatiable thirst for knowledge and ceaseless pursuit of excellence.

And so we conclude this chapter with eager anticipation for what lies ahead—a world where human ingenuity converges with artificial intelligence to unlock new frontiers previously unimaginable. Brace yourself, dear reader—for the future is now within our grasp!

# Chapter Six

# The Neural Networks Behind AI

**U**nraveling the Intricacies of Neural Networks

In the vast and ever-evolving landscape of Artificial Intelligence, one concept stands as a testament to our pursuit of replicating the complexity of the human brain - Neural Networks. Brace yourself, dear reader, for we are about to embark on a journey through the intricate labyrinth of these digital marvels that have forever altered the course of technology. Imagine if you will, a symphony of electric pulses cascading through an ethereal expanse. This is where neural networks come alive, dancing with an elegance that rivals even the most graceful ballet. Just as biological neurons fire and transmit signals within our own minds, artificial neurons within these networks intricately communicate with one another. It is this dance that allows machines to mimic human-like cognition and solve complex problems with astonishing precision.

The core essence of a neural network lies in its ability to learn from data patterns and make predictions based on that acquired knowledge. Picture it as an artist honing their craft - each stroke paints a broader picture until it becomes a masterpiece. Similarly, neural networks begin as blank canvases yearning for experience; they ingest vast amounts of data and gradually refine their understanding until they can seamlessly navigate and interpret complex information.

These digital marvels consist not only of individual artificial neurons but also interconnected layers that form a network structure resembling the intricate web spun by nature's arachnids. Each layer serves its purpose diligently - extracting features from input data in one layer before passing them on to subsequent layers for further analysis. It's akin to peeling back layers upon layers of enigmatic secrets until we reach enlightenment. Now, let us delve into this wondrous realm by exploring two fundamental types of neural networks: feedforward and recurrent networks.

In the grand tapestry woven by technological innovation, feedforward neural networks reign supreme as pioneers in machine learning. Much like water flowing downstream without any backward glance, information travels in a single direction within these networks. This unidirectional flow enables feedforward networks to excel at tasks such as image recognition, natural language processing, and even predicting stock market trends. Their simplicity belies their effectiveness, making them a cornerstone of modern AI.

But wait! There is another virtuoso waiting in the wings - the recurrent neural network. Picture it as a time traveler, for it possesses the unique ability to retain memory of past events. This opens up a world of possibilities where information from previous time steps can influence the current output, allowing recurrent networks to tackle sequential data with unparalleled finesse. From speech recognition to language translation, these mighty machines have revolutionized our understanding of temporal relationships.

As we bask in the radiance of these neural wonders, let us not forget their limitations and challenges that lie beneath their seemingly flawless veneer. Training neural networks requires vast amounts of data and computational resources - a feat that may seem daunting at first glance. Moreover, ensuring generalization beyond the boundaries of training data remains an ongoing pursuit for researchers worldwide.

Dear reader, we have traversed through the awe-inspiring realm of neural networks - those magnificent creations that mirror our own cognitive prowess. We have witnessed their mesmerizing dance within intricate layers and marveled at their ability to learn from vast oceans of data. But this journey is far from over; there are still uncharted territories waiting to be explored and new frontiers awaiting our arrival. With every passing day, humanity's understanding deepens as we continue to unlock the mysteries hidden within these digital masterpieces. So I implore you: embrace curiosity and venture forth into this wondrous world where Artificial Intelligence intertwines with human ingenuity. For it is through understanding that we shall truly grasp the limitless potential that lies within Neural Networks - an ever-evolving symphony orchestrating our future with unparalleled grace.

**Unraveling the Depths of Deep Learning**

In the ever-evolving landscape of artificial intelligence, a force of unparalleled magnitude emerges - deep learning. Welcome to a realm where neural networks delve into the depths of complexity, unraveling intricate patterns and unlocking the secrets that lie within. In this chapter, we embark on an exhilarating journey to explore the profound significance of deep learning in training these complex neural networks.

As we immerse ourselves in this captivating realm, it is crucial to grasp the essence of deep learning. At its core, deep learning is an approach that enables machines to learn directly from raw data without explicit programming instructions. Drawing inspiration from the human brain's intricate web of neurons and synapses, deep learning utilizes artificial neural networks with multiple hidden layers to process information in a hierarchical manner.

The allure of deep learning lies in its ability to tackle complex tasks that were once deemed impossible for traditional machine learning algorithms. From image and speech recognition to natural language processing and autonomous driving systems, these advanced neural networks have paved the way for unprecedented breakthroughs across diverse domains. To comprehend why deep learning holds such tremendous power, we must venture into its inner workings. Picture a vast network composed of interconnected nodes - neurons - each equipped with learnable parameters that adjust based on input signals. Through an iterative process called training or "learning," these neural networks refine their parameters by minimizing errors and optimizing performance.

One might wonder what sets apart deep learning from its predecessors. The answer lies within its remarkable capacity for abstraction and representation. By constructing multiple layers within a network architecture, each layer extracts increasingly complex features from raw data as it progresses deeper into the network hierarchy. This hierarchical representation allows for an unparalleled level of abstraction – akin to peeling back layers upon layers revealing deeper insights hidden beneath the surface. It is this ability that enables deep learning models to understand intricate patterns within datasets comprehensively.

As our understanding of deep learning grows, we begin to appreciate the immense potential it holds. The impact of deep learning resonates across various fields, revolutionizing industries and transforming the way we perceive artificial intelligence. In healthcare, deep learning models have demonstrated exceptional accuracy in diagnosing diseases from medical images, aiding doctors in making swift and accurate decisions.

In the realm of finance, these advanced neural networks provide unparalleled insights into market trends and patterns, empowering traders with predictive analytics to make informed investment choices. Moreover, deep learning has found its place in natural language processing applications such as machine translation and sentiment analysis, enabling seamless communication between individuals from different corners of the globe. As our journey through the realm of deep learning draws to a close, we are left awestruck by its tremendous influence on shaping our present and defining our future. Its ability to unravel complexities once deemed insurmountable has unlocked a world where machines can learn with astonishing accuracy and efficiency.

With each passing day, we witness new frontiers being conquered - boundaries pushed further by these exceptional neural networks. From deciphering ancient texts to generating artistic masterpieces, no challenge seems too daunting for the powerhouses of deep learning.

**The Wonders of Neural Networks in Image Recognition**

In this captivating chapter, we delve into the mesmerizing world of neural networks and their remarkable role in image recognition systems. Brace yourself for a thrilling journey as we unravel the secrets behind these powerful algorithms and witness how they transform mere pixels into profound understanding.

As we embark on this adventure, let us first comprehend the essence of neural networks. Picture a vast network of interconnected neurons, each pulsating with extraordinary vitality. These artificial counterparts to our brain's neurons possess an insatiable hunger for knowledge, yearning to decipher the intricacies hidden within every image. They tirelessly analyze patterns, shapes, colors, and textures until they unlock the true meaning concealed beneath.

The main purpose of employing neural networks in image recognition systems is to mimic the human brain's ability to perceive and understand visual information effortlessly. By employing layers upon layers of these artificial neurons, we create a complex web that can unravel even the most enigmatic visual puzzle. Imagine gazing upon a photograph—a serene landscape adorned with vibrant flowers dancing in the wind. To us humans, it may seem like an effortless task to identify these blossoms by their distinctive shapes and colors. However, for computers devoid of our innate understanding and intuition, it proves to be an arduous endeavor.

This is where neural networks step onto the stage as heroes adorned with capes woven from algorithms and powered by knowledge amassed through training data. They tirelessly learn from millions upon millions of images until their perception reaches unprecedented heights. The process begins by feeding vast amounts of labeled images into these neural networks—their digital sustenance. Layer by layer, each neuron analyzes specific features within these images—edges here, corners there—until collectively they form a comprehensive understanding.

With each passing iteration through this labyrinthine network of artificial intelligence lies growth—an exponential enhancement in accuracy and efficiency. Like a painter adding brushstrokes to an ever-evolving masterpiece, the neural network refines its ability to recognize patterns, grasping the essence of what makes an image truly unique.

But what lies at the heart of this incredible journey is an innovative technique known as deep learning. This revolutionary approach empowers neural networks with the capability to automatically learn and adapt from data, without being explicitly programmed. Through this process, these networks become nimble learners, adapting their understanding to tackle even the most complex visual challenges.

As we conclude this chapter on neural networks in image recognition systems, let us reflect upon the remarkable strides we have witnessed. From raw pixels to profound comprehension, these algorithms have taken us on a transformative odyssey through artificial intelligence's ever-expanding horizons. So next time you gaze upon a breathtaking photograph or marvel at a computer's ability to decipher imagery with unmatched precision, remember that it is the tireless work of neural networks that lies behind such wonders. The journey continues as we delve deeper into AI's vast landscape—uncovering its secrets one chapter at a time. Ride this wave of knowledge and immerse yourself in the enigmatic embrace of Understanding AI: A Comprehensive Guide for Beginners.

# Chapter Seven

# Ethical Considerations in AI

**U**nveiling the Shadows of Bias

In the vast realm of Artificial Intelligence, where minds and machines converge, a dark presence looms. It is a specter that haunts the algorithms we hold dear, casting its malevolent shadow on the marginalized communities it touches. This chapter unravels the intricate web of biased algorithms and delves into their profound impact on society. As we embark on this exploration, let us first grasp the essence of bias in AI algorithms. These algorithms possess a remarkable ability to learn from data and make autonomous decisions. But alas, they are not infallible; they carry within them echoes of human prejudice. Like an unseen force guiding their actions, bias seeps into their very fabric.

The implications are far-reaching, for these biased algorithms have the power to perpetuate discrimination against marginalized communities. Imagine a world where opportunities are determined by lines of code tainted with prejudice – a world where individuals face barriers due to race, gender, or socioeconomic status. One might wonder how such bias is embedded within these seemingly impartial systems. Well, my dear reader, it begins with the data upon which these algorithms are trained—the very lifeblood that courses through their digital veins. Data holds immense power in shaping AI algorithms; it molds them into instruments that reflect our own biases. If we feed them data tainted by historical injustices or societal prejudices, they will inevitably learn and mimic those biases in their actions.

Consider an algorithm used in hiring processes that has been trained on historical employment data predominantly favoring certain demographics over others. The algorithm may unknowingly perpetuate this bias by favoring candidates who fit within those established patterns while neglecting equally qualified individuals from marginalized backgrounds. But let us not despair! There is hope amidst this darkness—a glimmer of light shining through the cracks in these flawed systems. By acknowledging and understanding bias within AI algorithms, we can strive towards rectifying these injustices.

One approach is to foster diversity and inclusivity within the development of AI algorithms. By incorporating diverse perspectives into the creation process, we can mitigate the risks of biased outcomes. It is through collaboration and collective wisdom that we can build a more equitable future. Additionally, transparency and accountability are crucial in addressing bias. Algorithmic decision-making should not be shrouded in secrecy; rather, it should be open to scrutiny and oversight. Auditing algorithms for bias and implementing mechanisms for recourse will help restore trust in these systems.

To truly conquer bias in AI, we must also invest in education and awareness. By empowering individuals with knowledge about algorithmic bias, we equip them with the tools to challenge these systems when they perpetuate discrimination. Through education, we foster a society that questions and strives for fairness.

### The Ethical Tightrope of AI Privacy

In this riveting chapter, we delve into the intricate web of ethical concerns surrounding the ever-evolving realm of Artificial Intelligence (AI). Brace yourself, dear reader, for a thought-provoking exploration that will leave you questioning the very fabric of our technological landscape. As AI systems become increasingly omnipresent in our daily lives, safeguarding user privacy and protecting sensitive data emerge as paramount concerns. We find ourselves walking a tightrope between the remarkable capabilities of AI and the critical need to preserve personal privacy. How can we strike a delicate balance between progress and protection? Let us embark on this intellectual journey together.

At first glance, one might be tempted to marvel at the sheer brilliance of AI algorithms and their ability to sift through vast troves of data with unprecedented efficiency. However, beneath this mesmerizing facade lies an ethical conundrum that demands immediate attention. Imagine, if you will, an AI system capable of predicting an individual's behavior patterns based on their digital footprint—a seemingly harmless feat. Yet in doing so, are we not encroaching upon one's right to privacy? A chilling question indeed.

To fully grasp the gravity of these concerns, it is crucial to explore real-world examples where AI's insatiable appetite for data has crossed ethical boundaries. Take social media platforms as an illustration; they have become breeding grounds for invasive algorithms that mine personal information without remorse. Our online activities are meticulously tracked and analyzed—a sobering reality that leaves us vulnerable to exploitation by both corporate entities and ill-intentioned actors alike.

But fear not! For every challenge presents an opportunity for growth and transformation. As responsible stewards of technology in this digital age, it falls upon us to establish robust frameworks that prioritize user privacy above all else. Transparency becomes our guiding principle—a beacon shining brightly amidst a sea of uncertainty. To achieve this noble goal, stringent regulations must be put in place to protect personal data from falling into the wrong hands. We must advocate for the implementation of privacy-centric AI systems that operate within defined boundaries, ensuring user consent and granting individuals the right to control their own information. Only through these safeguards can we navigate the treacherous waters of AI with confidence and integrity. But let us not forget, dear reader, that ethics transcend mere regulations. They reside within each one of us, beckoning us to embrace our moral compasses when designing and deploying AI technologies. As creators and innovators, we possess an immense responsibility—a duty to weave ethical considerations into the very fabric of AI's existence.

This chapter serves as a clarion call—a wake-up call—to confront the ethical implications surrounding AI privacy head-on. We stand at a crossroads where our choices will shape the future landscape of technology and its impact on humanity. Let us seize this moment with unwavering resolve, forging a path that harmonizes progress with privacy protection. Together, we shall usher in an era where technological marvels coexist harmoniously with individual sovereignty—a future where understanding AI is synonymous with safeguarding human dignity.

## Transparency and Accountability in AI Development

In the intricate world of artificial intelligence (AI), where machines mimic human cognition, transparency and accountability serve as beacons of hope amidst the enigmatic depths. As we embark on this chapter, let us unravel the significance of transparency in AI development while delving into the crucial endeavor of holding its creators accountable for their creations. AI, with its boundless potential to transform industries and augment human capabilities, has become an indomitable force shaping our present and future. However, such power must not reside solely in the hands of creators without proper checks and balances. Just as sunlight dissolves darkness, transparency acts as a guiding light that illuminates the inner workings of AI systems.

One may ask, why does transparency matter? Is it not enough to marvel at AI's prowess from afar? Ah, my dear reader, understanding is key to embracing this technological marvel fully. When we comprehend how AI algorithms operate and make decisions, we empower ourselves to question biases or potential risks lurking beneath their digital veneer. Imagine a world where autonomous vehicles navigate our streets with imperceptible flaws hidden within their programming. Without transparency, these flaws may remain concealed until tragedy strikes. By shining a light on how these algorithms function—unveiling their inner workings—we enable public scrutiny that safeguards against unintended consequences.

Transparency goes hand-in-hand with accountability—a symbiotic relationship necessary for fostering trust between humans and machines. Imagine an architect constructing a magnificent building without being held accountable for structural integrity; chaos would reign supreme! Similarly, creators must bear responsibility for ensuring that their AI systems align with ethical standards and societal values.

To achieve true accountability in AI development, we must devise mechanisms that hold creators liable for any adverse repercussions caused by their creations. Just as authors are answerable for every word they pen onto paper, so too should developers face consequences for the impact their algorithms have on our lives. This accountability demands a framework that encompasses legal, ethical, and regulatory measures. Beyond the realm of accountability lies the pursuit of fairness. AI systems must not perpetuate biases or discriminate against certain groups. By embracing transparency, we can scrutinize algorithms for any prejudices they may harbor—ensuring a level playing field where every individual's rights and dignity are preserved.

Moreover, transparency acts as a catalyst for continuous improvement in AI systems. When creators open the doors to their algorithms' inner workings, experts and researchers can identify flaws, suggest enhancements, and collectively advance the field. Through this collaborative approach, we pave the way towards AI systems that are more robust, reliable, and trustworthy.

My dear reader, transparency is not an option but an imperative in AI development. By shedding light on its inner mechanisms and holding creators accountable for their creations, we forge a path towards trust and progress. Let us embark upon this journey together—unveiling the veil of secrecy that shrouds artificial intelligence—and embrace a future where humans and machines coexist harmoniously in symbiotic synergy.

And so I leave you with these words: let us be torchbearers in this quest for transparency—a beacon shining brightly amidst the labyrinthine corridors of artificial intelligence—an unwavering testament to our unwavering commitment to understanding and harnessing its transformative power. For it is through our collective efforts that we shall unravel the mysteries of AI—the ultimate union between human ingenuity and technological marvels—as it dances upon the precipice of limitless possibilities awaiting those who dare to dream.

# Chapter Eight

# Building Blocks of AI: Data and Algorithms

**T**he Data Dilemma

In the vast realm of artificial intelligence, where algorithms and neural networks dance to the tune of innovation, one crucial element stands tall, demanding our utmost attention - data quality. Oh, dear reader, let us embark on a journey into the intricate world of AI and unravel the enigma that is the relationship between data and success. As we delve into this chapter, we must grasp the essence of high-quality data as it intertwines with training effective AI models. Picture a sculptor crafting a masterpiece from an exquisite block of marble. Just as every chisel strike shapes its form, each byte of data molds the capabilities and potentiality of an AI system. The cornerstone lies in understanding that it is not merely about quantity but quality. A vast sea of irrelevant or inaccurate data can drown even the most advanced algorithms in confusion. The triumph lies in curating a dataset that sparkles with precision and relevance like diamonds glistening under moonlight.

Imagine, if you will, a self-driving car navigating treacherous roads with outdated maps or faulty sensor readings - disaster would surely ensue! It is through meticulous attention to detail that we ensure our AI creations can navigate through these digital landscapes unscathed. To comprehend why high-quality data reigns supreme in AI training, we must first explore its multifaceted nature. Picture yourself at a bustling marketplace filled with vendors peddling their wares - each stall represents a different aspect of your dataset: accuracy, completeness, consistency, timeliness.

Accuracy forms the bedrock upon which our AI models stand tall. Like an orchestra conductor seeking perfect harmony among musicians, accurate data harmonizes algorithmic predictions with reality itself. Without this accuracy as our guiding star, predictions become nothing more than whimsical fantasies dancing within lines of code. Completeness serves as another vital piece to this intricate puzzle. Just as missing puzzle pieces render an image incomplete and unsatisfying, gaps in our data can hinder the holistic understanding of patterns and relationships. It is through completeness that AI models gain the power to uncover hidden insights and make informed decisions.

Consistency, my dear reader, is the heartbeat of effective AI models. Imagine a symphony where musicians play at their own tempo without regard for one another - chaos would reign supreme! Similarly, inconsistent data can lead to erratic predictions and unreliable outcomes. Consistency paves the way for stability and reliability in the realm of artificial intelligence. Timeliness brings with it a sense of urgency - a recognition that relevance decays over time. Just as yesterday's news becomes today's forgotten whispers, outdated data fails to capture the ever-evolving nature of our world. To ensure AI systems remain adaptable and resilient, we must feed them with fresh nourishment from an ever-flowing stream of data.

Ah, dear reader, we have traversed through a tapestry woven with threads of accuracy, completeness, consistency, and timeliness. Yet our journey does not end here; for every step forward reveals new challenges on this winding path towards AI success. In this chapter lies an invitation to embrace the importance of high-quality data in training effective AI models. It is through this lens that we witness algorithms transform into marvels capable of deciphering complex problems and unlocking extraordinary potential.

### Unraveling the Enigmatic Art of Algorithm Design

In the vast realm of artificial intelligence, where machines mimic human intelligence and unlock the mysteries of complex problems, lies a fundamental cornerstone that propels these marvels forward. This chapter delves into the enigmatic art of algorithm design—a discipline that breathes life into AI applications by unveiling the principles behind robustness and efficiency. As we embark on this captivating journey through the intricacies of algorithmic design, imagine yourself as an architect constructing a grand cathedral, meticulously laying each brick with unparalleled precision. Just as every brick forms an integral part of the structure, each line of code in an algorithm plays a crucial role in shaping AI's potential.

Let us begin our exploration by unraveling one essential principle: clarity. Like a beacon amid foggy shores, clarity guides us towards designing algorithms that transcend complexity and embrace simplicity. When crafting algorithms for AI applications, clarity reigns supreme. It illuminates the path to efficiency and empowers us to create solutions that navigate intricate webs with grace. To master algorithmic design is to possess an intuitive understanding of efficiency—an elusive mistress who dances on a tightrope between speed and resource consumption. Efficiency paints strokes upon an algorithmic canvas—each stroke optimizing performance while minimizing cost. As you traverse this artistic landscape, remember that elegance resides not only in sophistication but also in parsimony.

Now let us venture into another dimension where adaptability reigns supreme—the realm of robustness. Robustness is akin to crafting a ship capable of weathering tempestuous seas without faltering—a vessel impervious to turbulent tides. In the domain of algorithms, robustness equips our creations with resilience against unforeseen circumstances; it shields them from crashing upon rocky shores when faced with imperfect data or unexpected variables. As twilight gives way to dawn, let us unveil another secret ingredient within this captivating brew—creativity. Like a master painter, an algorithm designer must possess the gift of imagination. For algorithms are not mere mechanical constructs; they are the embodiment of human ingenuity. Through creativity, we infuse our algorithms with a touch of artistry, enabling them to transcend limitations and explore uncharted territories.

Now that we have unraveled some of the key principles within algorithm design, let us embark on a practical journey—an expedition into the world of AI applications. Along this path, we shall witness algorithms unlock the secrets hidden within vast datasets, breathing life into intelligent systems that can discern patterns and make informed decisions.

Let us bask in the intoxicating aura of algorithmic design—a realm where clarity dances with efficiency, robustness navigates turbulent waters, and creativity paints mesmerizing landscapes. As you immerse yourself in this world brimming with possibilities, remember that every line of code holds transformative potential—a brushstroke that shapes our technological future. For in understanding AI lies not merely knowledge but also an invitation—to join a community that pushes boundaries and unlocks doors once thought impassable. So embrace this opportunity with unwavering curiosity and let your imagination soar as you embark upon this exhilarating voyage through the realms of artificial intelligence.

### Unveiling the Secrets of Data Privacy and Security

In a digital world fueled by technological advancements, where the lines between reality and virtuality blur, it becomes imperative to delve into the intricate realm of data privacy and security. As we continue our journey in unraveling the enigmatic depths of AI development, we now find ourselves standing at the precipice of an abyss filled with sensitive information that demands safeguarding. Brace yourself, dear reader, for we are about to embark on a quest to comprehend the importance of protecting these treasures amidst the ever-evolving landscape of artificial intelligence.

Picture this: A sprawling metropolis bustling with life, where each individual is intertwined with technology on an unprecedented scale. From smartphones that seem to know our every desire to smart homes that cater to our every need, our lives have become intricately interwoven with digital platforms. But beneath this seemingly utopian facade lies a vast ocean of data; a treasure trove housing our deepest secrets and most intimate moments. Yet, as AI continues its relentless march forward, fueled by countless lines of code and mind-boggling algorithms, it is crucial that we pause for a momentary reflection on what lies at stake. Our very identities are at risk - identities molded from bits and bytes - vulnerable to cyber threats lurking in shadowy corners.

Data breaches have become alarmingly routine occurrences in recent years; behemoth corporations left reeling from cyberattacks as personal information falls into malicious hands. The consequences are far-reaching - financial ruin for some, shattered reputations for others - all stemming from a lackadaisical approach towards data privacy. But let us not despair! In understanding AI's profound role in shaping our future endeavors, we must acknowledge its inherent potential alongside its inherent perils. For within every challenge lies an opportunity; an opportunity to fortify ourselves against those who would seek to exploit our vulnerabilities.

When it comes to data privacy and security, ignorance is not bliss; it is a Pandora's box waiting to be opened. As we traverse this complex landscape, it becomes evident that the responsibility lies not only in the hands of individuals but also in the collective consciousness of society as a whole. Governments must enact stringent regulations, corporations must prioritize transparency and accountability, and individuals must become stewards of their own digital footprints. In this ever-shifting paradigm, encryption emerges as a stalwart defender against prying eyes. Imagine an impenetrable fortress erected around our most valued possessions - our data shielded by layers upon layers of cryptographic algorithms. Encryption is the key to preserving privacy in an age where digital footprints are etched indelibly upon the digital canvas. But encryption alone cannot bear the burden of safeguarding our digital existence; for within its protective embrace lies an inherent dichotomy - a delicate balance between privacy and utility. We find ourselves grappling with ethical quandaries as we weigh the scales between protecting sensitive information and harnessing its power for societal progress.

As we wander through this labyrinthine realm, it is crucial to remember that data privacy and security are not mere buzzwords or fleeting concerns. They are pillars upon which trust is built - trust between individuals, trust between institutions, and trust between humans and machines alike. And so, dear reader, let us embark on this arduous yet necessary journey together - a journey that will shape not only our understanding of AI but also our very existence in the digital age. Let us forge ahead with unwavering determination to safeguard what is rightfully ours while embracing the boundless potential that AI holds. For within these paradoxical depths lie both perilous pitfalls and extraordinary possibilities awaiting those who dare to tread this path less traveled.

And thus concludes our exploration into Data Privacy and Security amidst AI development – a chapter filled with intrigue and contemplation; urging us to recognize the significance of safeguarding sensitive information in this brave new world. As we bid adieu to this chapter, dear reader, let us pause for a moment of reflection and brace ourselves for the adventures that lie ahead.

# Chapter Nine

# AI in Everyday Life

**A** **Symphony of Convenience and Ingenuity**

In the modern world, where technology reigns supreme, our homes have become a canvas upon which innovation and convenience paint their masterpieces. Virtual assistants and smart home technologies have revolutionized the way we interact with our living spaces, transforming them into havens of efficiency and functionality. Prepare to embark on a journey through the realm of virtual assistants and smart homes, where automation meets elegance, and convenience dances hand in hand with ingenuity.

As you step through the threshold of this chapter, be prepared to be dazzled by a symphony of cutting-edge technologies that converge to create an orchestra of convenience. Imagine waking up in the morning to the dulcet tones of your favorite music gently wafting through your home, all orchestrated by a virtual assistant that knows your every preference. With a simple command like "Good morning," your home springs into action - curtains effortlessly draw open to reveal the world outside, lights gradually illuminate each room as if awakening from slumber, and even your coffee pot begins brewing that perfect cup of joe.

But it doesn't stop there; oh no! Smart homes are not merely about waking up in style; they are about living in harmony with technology that seamlessly integrates into our daily lives. Picture this: you arrive home after a long day at work, burdened by fatigue and stress. As you step inside your sanctuary, sensors detect your presence and adjust the ambiance accordingly - soft lighting envelops you like a warm embrace while soothing music fills the air. In this interconnected web of technological marvels lies the heart and soul: virtual assistants. These digital companions possess an intelligence rivaled only by their human creators - or perhaps even surpassing it. With names like Alexa, Siri, or Google Assistant on their digital lips, they respond eagerly to your beckoning call for assistance.

"Alexa," you say with conviction as if summoning an ancient deity, "dim the lights and play my favorite playlist." In an instant, your surroundings transform to match your desires. Shadows lengthen, casting a cozy glow as if embracing you in their warm embrace. The harmonious tunes of your preferred soundtrack fill every corner of your abode, as if orchestrated by the very hands of Beethoven himself.

But virtual assistants do not limit themselves to mere entertainment or ambience; they extend their reach into every aspect of our lives. From managing our calendars and providing weather updates to ordering groceries and controlling the temperature, these digital genies grant our wishes with a mere utterance. "Hey Siri," you inquire with curiosity dancing in your eyes, "what's on my schedule for tomorrow?" With a gentle voice that echoes from unseen speakers, Siri dutifully recites your itinerary for the coming day. Your mind is put at ease as you realize that no detail has been overlooked - everything from important meetings to personal appointments is accounted for.

As we traverse the landscape of virtual assistants and smart homes, we are met with an ever-expanding array of possibilities. These technologies hold within them the promise of a future where convenience is not merely an afterthought but embedded into the very fabric of our existence. But let us remember that amid this dance between artificial intelligence and human ingenuity lies a delicate balance. As we surrender more aspects of our lives to automation, let us not forget the importance of retaining our personal touch - for it is in these subtleties that true beauty resides.

So dear reader, embrace this symphony of convenience and ingenuity; let its melodious notes guide you through a world where technology serves not as a master but as an unwavering ally. And may your journey through virtual assistants and smart homes be one filled with awe-inspiring discoveries and harmonious integration into every fiber of your being. For in this realm lies endless potential - one where artistry and automation join forces to create a symphony that resonates with the very essence of what it means to be human.

### Unveiling the Magic of Personalized Recommendations

In the vast realm of technology, where algorithms dance with data and machines whisper secrets of human desires, lies a captivating phenomenon known as personalized recommendations. Brace yourself, dear readers, for we are about to embark on a journey that will unravel the intricate web woven by AI-driven recommendation systems. Prepare to be enchanted as we explore how these digital sorcerers enhance user experiences in entertainment, shopping, and beyond.

Imagine stepping into a world where every film you watch, every song you listen to, every book you read is carefully tailored to your unique tastes. This world exists at our fingertips, thanks to the marvels of AI-driven recommendation systems. These omnipresent wizards analyze vast amounts of data - your browsing history, preferences, and even social interactions - conjuring up enchanting suggestions that cater specifically to you. The magic begins when these recommendation systems cast their spell over streaming platforms such as Netflix or Spotify. With a flick of their digital wands, they delve deep into their treasure troves of content and unearth hidden gems that align perfectly with your interests. No longer shall you wander aimlessly through countless titles; instead, these mystical algorithms will guide you towards cinematic masterpieces or soul-stirring melodies that resonate with your very being.

But the wonders do not cease there! Shopping experiences are also touched by this ethereal magic. Picture this: as you peruse an online store in search of the perfect pair of shoes or that elusive vintage vinyl record for your collection, AI-driven recommendation systems work tirelessly behind the scenes. They analyze your past purchases and browsing patterns with an uncanny precision akin to a clairvoyant reading tea leaves. These digital soothsayers then weave their recommendations seamlessly into your shopping journey – suggesting similar products that might pique your interest or even predicting items you never knew existed but now desperately crave. It's as if they have read your mind, teasing out your deepest desires and presenting them to you on a virtual silver platter.

Now, dear readers, let us delve deeper into the inner workings of these enigmatic recommendation systems. They are not mere gatekeepers of content or purveyors of products. No, they are much more than that. These AI-driven wizards harness the power of machine learning, constantly adapting and evolving as they gather more data about your preferences and behaviors. Their algorithms learn from your choices - the films you rate highly, the songs you skip, the items you add to cart but never purchase - and use this knowledge to refine their spells. With each interaction, they grow wiser and more adept at predicting what will captivate your heart and ignite your imagination.

But beware! The seductive allure of personalized recommendations comes with a caveat. As these digital enchanters become ever more skilled at understanding our desires, we must remember to question their influence. Are we truly discovering new experiences or merely existing within an echo chamber that reinforces our existing tastes? Let us reflect upon the profound impact they have on our lives. They whisk us away from mundanity and introduce us to worlds we may never have ventured into alone. But amidst the wonderment lies a call for discernment – let us embrace their offerings while maintaining a critical eye.

### The Unwavering Guardians of Our Highways

The sun hung low in the sky as the autonomous vehicle glided effortlessly down the open road. This marvel of modern technology, guided by the unseen hand of artificial intelligence, had become a symbol of our relentless pursuit for progress. With each passing year, these intelligent machines have become more prevalent on our roads, promising a future where accidents are but distant memories. In this chapter, we embark on a thrilling journey into the world of autonomous vehicles and delve into the pivotal role that AI plays in ensuring their safety and efficiency. As we peel back the layers of this technological marvel, we unveil an intricate web of algorithms and sensors working harmoniously to protect us from harm.

At the heart of every autonomous vehicle lies a complex neural network capable of processing vast amounts of data in real-time. This intricate brain, trained through countless hours of machine learning, is designed to make split-second decisions that keep us safe on our journeys. It is here that AI steps onto the stage as both guardian and conductor, orchestrating a symphony that balances efficiency with safety. Imagine for a moment being behind the wheel as you approach an intersection bustling with activity. The traffic lights change at lightning speed, demanding immediate action. In this crucial moment when milliseconds can spell disaster or salvation, it is AI that takes charge. Through its omniscient gaze upon sensors embedded throughout the vehicle and its tireless analysis of incoming data streams, it calculates precise trajectories and timing to navigate through this intricate dance with utmost precision.

But what happens when unforeseen obstacles appear? A pedestrian stepping out unexpectedly or an animal darting across our path? Fear not! For within every autonomous vehicle resides an AI system primed to identify potential hazards before they even materialize. Its virtual eyes see beyond human limitations and its neural pathways can decipher patterns imperceptible to mortal minds. The safety net woven by AI goes beyond mere obstacle detection. It extends its reach to encompass predictive analysis and risk assessment. By constantly monitoring road conditions, traffic patterns, and even weather forecasts, AI can anticipate potential dangers and adjust its driving strategy accordingly. This uncanny ability to foresee the future allows autonomous vehicles to adapt seamlessly to changing circumstances, ensuring a smooth and secure journey for all.

As we marvel at the capabilities of AI in safeguarding our highways, it is vital to acknowledge the ongoing efforts in research and development. Brilliant minds from around the world are tirelessly working to enhance these intelligent systems further. Their mission: to create a future where autonomous vehicles are not only safer but also more efficient. In this quest for efficiency, AI plays a vital role in optimizing energy consumption and traffic flow. Imagine a world where roads teem with self-driving cars seamlessly merging, accelerating, and decelerating in perfect synchrony; where traffic congestion is but an archaic relic of the past. Through advanced algorithms that analyze data from multiple sources simultaneously, AI can orchestrate this symphony of motion, ensuring optimal fuel usage while minimizing travel time.

With each passing day, the bond between artificial intelligence and autonomous vehicles grows stronger. Their partnership holds immense promise for our collective future—a future where accidents become a distant memory and transportation becomes safer than ever before. And so we conclude yet another captivating chapter on our journey through understanding AI. In this installment, we have witnessed firsthand how AI assumes the role of protector and conductor within the realm of autonomous vehicles—guiding us towards an era marked by both safety and efficiency.

But dear reader, let us not rest on our laurels! For there are still untold wonders waiting to be unveiled within this vast landscape of artificial intelligence. Join me as we continue our exploration into uncharted territories—a voyage that promises endless revelations about the intricacies of understanding AI!

# Chapter Ten

# The Future of AI: Trends and Possibilities

**The Astonishing Evolution of Natural Language Processing**

In the realm of artificial intelligence, a wondrous phenomenon has emerged, captivating the minds of researchers and enthusiasts alike. This chapter shall delve into the mesmerizing advancements in Natural Language Processing (NLP), unearthing the latest developments that have enabled AI to comprehend and generate language akin to human eloquence. Prepare to embark on a journey through the ever-evolving landscape of NLP, where machines strive to grasp the essence of our linguistic prowess.

As we traverse this realm, it is imperative to understand that NLP encompasses a multitude of techniques and algorithms aimed at bridging the gap between human communication and machine comprehension. Through this chapter's exploration, we shall witness how AI has transcended mere syntax and grammar rules, venturing into semantic understanding and contextual interpretation. The genesis of NLP can be traced back to rule-based approaches that relied upon predefined patterns and linguistic rules. However, as technology evolved at an exponential pace, these rudimentary methods paved way for more sophisticated models fueled by machine learning. Enter deep learning – a paradigm shift that revolutionized NLP as we know it today.

One monumental breakthrough within this paradigm was the advent of word embeddings. These transformative representations unlocked new dimensions in language understanding by capturing semantic relationships between words. As if awakening from a slumber, AI began discerning associations beyond surface-level meanings with astonishing accuracy. But let us not rest upon these laurels; for there is yet more marvel to behold within our journey through NLP's evolution. Enter recurrent neural networks (RNNs), instrumental in endowing machines with sequential memory and context sensitivity. Equipped with long short-term memory (LSTM) units or their variants, RNNs became adept at comprehending nuanced dependencies within textual data.

Yet another milestone manifested itself in the form of attention mechanisms – an innovation that bestowed AI with selective focus akin to our own cognitive processes. By selectively attending to relevant parts of a sentence, models gained an understanding of context and improved their ability to generate coherent responses. The rise of transformer architectures, spearheaded by the groundbreaking Transformer model, further elevated the prowess of attention mechanisms, birthing powerful language models such as GPT-3.

With these remarkable advancements at our disposal, AI has transcended the boundaries of deciphering human language and embarked upon the realm of language generation. Through generative models like OpenAI's GPT-3, machines can now fabricate text that mirrors human expression with an unprecedented level of fidelity. While not devoid of imperfections, these models are capable of producing eloquent prose that often leaves readers astounded by their authenticity. Let us marvel at the immense progress made in enabling AI to comprehend and generate human-like language. From rule-based systems to deep learning architectures and generative models, each milestone has propelled us closer to a future where machines will converse with us effortlessly – their linguistic virtuosity rivaling our own.

But remember, dear reader: while these advancements may appear miraculous on the surface, they are but tools in our quest for understanding artificial intelligence. It is we who must wield them responsibly and shape a world where technology serves as an ally rather than an adversary.

**The Revolution of AI in Healthcare Innovations**

In the realm of modern medicine, a revolution is brewing. A revolution fueled by the boundless possibilities and unwavering potential of Artificial Intelligence (AI). It is a revolution that promises to transform healthcare as we know it, ushering in an era of personalized medicine, groundbreaking diagnostics, and unparalleled healthcare management. In this chapter, we embark on a journey through the emerging trends in using AI for healthcare innovations. The human body, with its intricacies and complexities, has long puzzled even the most brilliant minds. But now, armed with the power of AI, scientists and medical professionals are decoding nature's enigma like never before. Imagine a world where diseases can be diagnosed with pinpoint accuracy, treatments can be tailored to individual needs, and patient outcomes can be optimized beyond imagination. This is not mere fantasy; this is the reality that AI in healthcare innovations brings forth.

At the forefront of this revolution lies personalized medicine - an approach that acknowledges the uniqueness of each individual's genetic makeup and tailors treatments accordingly. By leveraging AI algorithms to analyze vast amounts of genomic data, scientists are unlocking the secrets hidden within our DNA. With this knowledge at their fingertips, they can design targeted therapies that address specific genetic mutations or predispositions. But personalized medicine doesn't stop at genetics alone. AI has also found its way into diagnostic tools that are changing the landscape of disease detection. Take radiology as an example - traditionally reliant on human interpretation of medical images such as X-rays or MRIs. Now imagine machines capable of quickly analyzing these images with unrivaled precision and accuracy. Thanks to deep learning algorithms trained on vast datasets comprising thousands upon thousands of medical images, AI-powered diagnostic tools are becoming indispensable assets for medical professionals worldwide.

Beyond diagnostics and treatment lies perhaps one of the most critical aspects of healthcare - management itself. As hospitals grapple with ever-increasing patient loads and limited resources, AI offers a glimmer of hope. Through the analysis of vast amounts of data, AI algorithms can identify patterns and trends that may elude human observation. This allows for more efficient resource allocation, improved patient scheduling, and better decision-making overall.

Picture a hospital where AI seamlessly integrates with electronic health records, constantly monitoring patient vitals and alerting healthcare providers to any alarming changes. Imagine a system where predictive analytics can anticipate disease outbreaks or identify high-risk patients before they even show symptoms. The possibilities are endless. However, as with any revolution, challenges and ethical considerations abound. Ensuring the privacy and security of patient data remains paramount in an era where AI relies heavily on access to personal information. Additionally, the integration of AI into healthcare must be accompanied by robust regulations to safeguard against potential biases or misinterpretations.

We find ourselves on the precipice of a new era in healthcare - an era characterized by personalized medicine, groundbreaking diagnostics, and unparalleled healthcare management powered by the revolutionary force that is Artificial Intelligence. The impact of AI in healthcare innovations cannot be overstated; it holds the promise to elevate medical care to unprecedented heights.

### AI's Green Revolution

In the vast realm of technological advancements, one phenomena stands out as a beacon of hope amidst the chaos and uncertainty that plagues our planet - Artificial Intelligence. While often associated with robots and automation, AI has transcended these limited expectations and emerged as a powerful tool in combating some of the most pressing environmental challenges we face today. As we delve into the captivating world of AI's environmental applications, brace yourself for an awe-inspiring journey where innovation meets sustainability. Prepare to witness how this remarkable technology is harnessing its potential to tackle climate change and revolutionize resource management.

Picture this: a once barren landscape now teeming with life, a symphony of vibrant colors dancing in harmony with nature's rhythm. This transformation, made possible by AI-driven algorithms, breathes new life into our fragile ecosystems. By analyzing vast amounts of data collected from satellites, weather stations, and sensors deployed worldwide, machine learning algorithms can predict weather patterns with unprecedented accuracy. Armed with this knowledge, scientists can devise strategies to mitigate the effects of climate change on vulnerable regions.

But it doesn't stop there. The power of AI extends beyond mere predictions; it empowers us to take proactive measures for a sustainable future. Imagine an intelligent grid that optimizes energy distribution based on real-time demand and supply analysis. With every watt harnessed efficiently and wastage minimized to almost nothingness, we inch closer towards achieving energy utopia. Resource scarcity has always been a dark cloud looming over humanity's collective conscience. However, through AI's lens of innovation and efficiency optimization lies a glimmering ray of hope. Smart agriculture systems equipped with machine learning algorithms monitor soil moisture levels and nutrient content in real-time while providing tailored recommendations for optimal crop growth conditions.

Beyond land-based solutions lie uncharted waters teeming with possibilities - quite literally! Marine ecosystems are under immense pressure due to pollution and overfishing; however, AI unleashes its potential to safeguard our oceans. Autonomous underwater drones equipped with AI algorithms can detect and monitor harmful algal blooms, preventing the devastating consequences they have on marine life.

As we explore further into this realm of environmental applications, it becomes evident that AI is not just a tool but a catalyst for change. It unifies data from various sources and transforms it into actionable insights, empowering decision-makers with the knowledge needed to make informed choices. However, with great power comes great responsibility. Ethical considerations must be at the forefront of these technological advancements. As we develop sophisticated AI systems, we must ensure transparency and accountability in their decision-making processes. The development of ethical frameworks and regulations will pave the way for responsible AI deployment, ensuring that our planet's well-being remains paramount.

The marriage between artificial intelligence and environmental conservation has given birth to a new era - an era where innovation meets sustainability in perfect harmony. The potential of AI to address climate change and revolutionize resource management is nothing short of remarkable. From predicting weather patterns to optimizing energy distribution and transforming agriculture practices, AI proves itself as an invaluable ally in safeguarding our planet's future. Let us embark on this green revolution together; let us embrace the boundless potential of Artificial Intelligence as we strive towards a more sustainable world - one algorithm at a time.

# Chapter Eleven

# Getting Started: Practical AI for Beginners

**E**xploring the Digital Realm of AI Education

In this digital age, where knowledge is a mere click away, embarking on an educational journey has never been more accessible. As we dive deeper into the realm of artificial intelligence, it becomes imperative to equip ourselves with the tools and resources necessary to navigate this intricate landscape. Fear not, dear reader, for I shall guide you through a curated list of online platforms and courses that will ignite your passion for AI and propel you towards greatness.

Imagine yourself as an intrepid explorer traversing the vast digital expanse. With every step you take, new frontiers unfold before your very eyes. The first stop on our journey is the illustrious "AI University," a virtual sanctuary for knowledge-seekers like yourself. Here, esteemed professors from prestigious institutions around the globe converge to share their wisdom in captivating lectures that transport you into the heart of AI's inner workings. As we venture further into this digital abyss, we encounter "AI Academy," an interactive platform akin to a bustling marketplace filled with knowledge merchants peddling their wares. Here, one can indulge in tutorials that cater specifically to beginners like yourself - stepping stones towards understanding complex concepts in bite-sized portions.

But wait! Our odyssey does not end there; it merely gains momentum as we stumble upon "AI Mastermind." This unique platform offers a collaborative environment where individuals passionate about AI come together to solve real-world problems through teamwork and innovation. Picture yourself amidst a vibrant community of like-minded enthusiasts exchanging ideas and pushing the boundaries of what is possible.

No exploration would be complete without unearthing hidden gems along the way. In our quest for knowledge, we stumble upon "AIpedia," an online encyclopedia dedicated solely to demystifying every aspect of AI. Here lies a treasure trove of articles written by industry experts who distill complex theories into digestible prose - transforming esoteric concepts into palatable knowledge. As the sun sets on our expedition, we find solace in "AI Café," a virtual gathering place where AI aficionados come to discuss, debate, and share their insights. Engage in lively conversations with individuals who possess a burning passion for AI, and allow yourself to be captivated by the intellectual prowess that permeates this digital haven. I implore you to embrace the vast ocean of possibilities that lie before you. The platforms and courses I have presented are but stepping stones on your path towards AI enlightenment. With each click and keystroke, you inch closer to unraveling the mysteries of this enigmatic realm.

Remember, dear reader, that knowledge is not a stagnant entity but a living force that thrives on curiosity and exploration. Embrace the digital realm of AI education with open arms and an insatiable hunger for understanding. Let your journey be one of constant growth as you unlock doors previously unimaginable. In the words of Robert Frost: "Two roads diverged in a wood...I took the one less traveled by, And that has made all the difference." May your path be paved with wisdom and may your endeavors shape not only your own destiny but also redefine what it means to comprehend artificial intelligence.

## Unleashing the Power of AI: Beginner-Friendly Projects

In a world where Artificial Intelligence (AI) reigns supreme, the opportunity to dabble in its wonders has never been more accessible. Welcome, dear reader, to the realm of Simple AI Projects! Within these pages, we shall embark on a journey that will ignite your curiosity and empower you with the knowledge and skills to create your own AI marvels. Are you ready to dive headfirst into the thrilling domain of AI experimentation? Excellent! Before we proceed, let us set our intentions straight. This chapter aims to provide you, dear reader, with a roadmap towards mastering beginner-friendly AI projects that encourage hands-on learning and experimentation.

Now that our purpose is clear as crystal, let us venture forth and explore the magnificent possibilities that lie within our grasp. Imagine breathing life into your very own chatbot—a digital companion who listens attentively and responds with uncanny intelligence. Picture yourself delving into computer vision—an enchanting realm where machines discern objects from images or even detect emotions from facial expressions. The possibilities are boundless!

To bring these imaginings to life requires an understanding of the foundational concepts behind AI. Fear not! We shall traverse this complex landscape together, hand in hand. With each step along this path of discovery, we will unravel concepts such as machine learning algorithms, neural networks, and deep learning models—unveiling their secrets one layer at a time. Once equipped with this knowledge arsenal, it is time for you to roll up your sleeves and get your hands dirty in the fascinating world of coding. Fear not if you lack prior programming experience! With user-friendly platforms like TensorFlow or PyTorch at your disposal—accompanied by detailed documentation—you'll be weaving lines of code like a seasoned programmer in no time.

Now comes the thrilling part—the projects themselves! Brace yourself for an exhilarating journey as we explore three remarkable AI projects, tailored specifically for beginners like yourself. Each project will provide you with a unique opportunity to apply your newfound knowledge and witness the magic of AI unfold before your very eyes.

Project #1: Chatbot Companion

Step into the realm of conversational AI as we build a chatbot companion from scratch. With the power of natural language processing and machine learning algorithms, your chatbot will evolve into an intelligent conversationalist. Engage in delightful conversations, seek advice, or simply enjoy its witty banter.

Project #2: Image Recognition Wizardry

Unleash the power of computer vision as we delve into the captivating world of image recognition. Through carefully crafted neural networks, you will teach machines to identify objects, recognize faces, or even detect emotions hidden within pixelated portraits. Prepare to witness the fusion of art and technology!

Project #3: Sentiment Analysis Sorcery

Immerse yourself in the realm of emotion detection as we explore sentiment analysis. By analyzing textual data using powerful deep learning models, you'll gain insights into people's emotions—unleashing a world where words become windows to one's soul. Unlock secrets hidden within sentences and harness their emotional essence.

As our journey through these projects draws to a close, remember that this chapter is merely one stepping stone on your path towards mastering AI. The road ahead may be filled with challenges; however, armed with newfound knowledge and an unyielding passion for exploration, you possess all that is necessary to conquer even the most formidable obstacles.

Dear reader, embrace this momentous occasion! Embrace your innate curiosity and unleash it upon these beginner-friendly AI projects—projects that shall ignite a fire within you that can never be extinguished. Harness the power of AI; let it guide you towards uncharted territories where dreams are transformed into reality.

**Uniting Minds in the Realm of AI Brilliance**

In the vast expanse of knowledge that is the field of Artificial Intelligence, one cannot underestimate the sheer power and potential that lies within the connections we forge with fellow enthusiasts. While our journey thus far has delved into the intricacies and wonders of AI, it is now time to embark on a new chapter, one that emphasizes the importance of joining AI communities and networking with like-minded individuals and professionals.

Imagine a world where minds intertwine, ideas collide, and innovation surges through collective brilliance. This is precisely what awaits you when you take that leap into the realm of AI communities. These vibrant networks are not merely gatherings; they are cauldrons bubbling with creativity and opportunity. As humans, we thrive on connection. We yearn for meaningful interactions that ignite our passions and push us to new heights. And in this age of technological marvels, we have been granted an unparalleled opportunity to connect with individuals who share our fervor for artificial intelligence.

Within these communities lie experts from various disciplines - mathematicians, computer scientists, engineers - all converging to unravel the mysteries of this captivating domain. Through lively discussions, collaborative projects, and shared experiences, these communities become fertile grounds for personal growth as well as professional advancement. But why should you join an AI community? Allow me to paint a vivid picture for you:

Picture yourself entering a room pulsating with intellectual energy. The air crackles with anticipation as each member prepares to contribute their unique perspective. Conversations ebb and flow like currents in a mighty river; ideas surge forth like waves crashing upon distant shores. As you immerse yourself in these conversations – absorbing knowledge like a sponge – you witness firsthand how diverse backgrounds converge into a symphony of thought-provoking insights. You engage in spirited debates about cutting-edge algorithms or discuss innovative applications that could revolutionize entire industries.

In these AI communities, you'll find mentors who have traversed the same path you're embarking on. They are beacons of wisdom, guiding you through the labyrinthine complexities of machine learning, natural language processing, and neural networks. Their experiences become stepping stones to your own success. Moreover, these communities offer a sanctuary for collaboration. Assembling a team with complementary skills can propel your endeavors to unforeseen heights. Together, you can tackle grand challenges that may have seemed insurmountable alone. The sheer power of collective intelligence ignites a fire within; an unyielding drive to push boundaries and redefine what is possible.

But let us not forget the intangible beauty that emerges from such connections – the friendships forged amidst shared passions. In these communities, bonds are woven as tightly as the threads of a tapestry. Friendships blossom and flourish in this fertile soil of mutual understanding and respect. As we conclude this chapter on AI communities and networking, I implore you to take that first step towards joining these vibrant ecosystems. Seek out conferences, meetups, or online forums where individuals gather to discuss their love for all things AI. Immerse yourself in this world where knowledge flows freely like a river carving its course through untouched landscapes.

Remember, dear reader: united we stand at the precipice of innovation; divided we stumble in stagnation's shadow. Let us unite our minds in this realm of AI brilliance and forge ahead into an era where artificial intelligence transcends its potential to revolutionize every aspect of our lives.

# Chapter Twelve

# Empowering the Future: Your Role in the AI Landscape

**E**xploring the Vast Landscape of AI Careers

In a world driven by unprecedented advancements in technology, the realm of Artificial Intelligence (AI) stands as a captivating frontier, offering a multitude of career opportunities. As we embark on this chapter, dear reader, prepare to witness the breathtaking panorama that awaits those who dare to delve into the enigmatic depths of AI. From unraveling complex algorithms to pondering the ethical implications of intelligent machines, this chapter shall illuminate your path towards an illustrious career in AI.

Step into the realm of data science, where hidden treasures lie concealed within vast oceans of information. Here, in this ever-expanding universe of data analysis and interpretation, lies an opportunity for you to become an alchemist—an alchemist who transforms raw data into priceless insights. Embrace your inner detective as you meticulously uncover patterns and trends, extracting valuable knowledge that fuels innovation across industries. The power to revolutionize decision-making processes awaits those who embark on this exhilarating journey.

But wait! The allure of AI does not end with data science alone. Prepare yourself for a riveting exploration into machine learning—a domain where algorithms learn from experience and evolve through continuous adaptation. Picture yourself at the helm of cutting-edge technologies that enable autonomous vehicles to navigate bustling streets or empower virtual assistants to comprehend our desires with uncanny precision. This captivating field beckons pioneers who possess both scientific acumen and creative intuition—a harmonious marriage between logic and imagination.

Venture further along our odyssey through AI careers until you stumble upon natural language processing—the mystical artform that grants machines the ability to understand human language in all its nuanced glory. Imagine shaping conversational agents capable of engaging us in meaningful dialogue or crafting language models that generate prose indistinguishable from human authorship. A symphony composed by words awaits those audacious enough to tame their linguistic prowess alongside technological wizardry.

As we delve deeper into uncharted territories within the AI landscape, we encounter a crucial facet that demands our unwavering attention—the ethical implications of intelligent machines. In this era of AI enlightenment, we must grapple with profound questions: How can we ensure fairness and inclusivity in AI systems? Can we safeguard against biases that may perpetuate discrimination? Ethical AI practitioners rise to the occasion, weaving morality into the very fabric of technological advancements. They act as guardians, guiding us towards a future where human values harmoniously coexist with artificial intelligence.

Dear reader, the vast expanse of AI careers stretches beyond what words can adequately capture. From computer vision to robotics, from augmented reality to deep learning—the possibilities are boundless. Each path presents its own challenges and rewards, awaiting those bold enough to embark on this grand adventure. As we near the conclusion of this chapter, let us not bid farewell in a conventional manner. Instead, let us take a moment to reflect upon our journey thus far—a journey that has divulged only a fraction of what lies ahead. The realm of AI beckons you, dear reader, to embark upon an odyssey filled with intellectual stimulation and profound impact—a voyage where human ingenuity converges with machine capabilities.

**Unleashing the Power of Continuous Learning**

In the ever-evolving realm of Artificial Intelligence, staying ahead of the curve is not just a mere aspiration; it is an absolute necessity. As we delve into the final chapters of "Understanding AI: A Comprehensive Guide for Beginners," we find ourselves at a crossroads, where the relentless pursuit of knowledge becomes our guiding light. In this chapter, we embark on a journey to unlock the secrets of continuous learning strategies that will enable you to navigate this dynamic field with finesse and adaptability.

The first step towards embracing continuous learning lies in cultivating a growth mindset. Approach each day with an insatiable curiosity, ready to explore new horizons and challenge conventional wisdom. Understand that failure is not an obstacle but rather a stepping stone towards progress. Embrace setbacks as opportunities for growth and use them as fuel to ignite your passion for unraveling the mysteries of AI. To embark on this transformative voyage, one must avail themselves of a vast array of resources that cater to every facet of AI exploration. Online courses, immersive boot camps, and interactive tutorials are just some examples that can help immerse oneself in the world of artificial intelligence. The internet has become an expansive treasure trove brimming with invaluable knowledge waiting to be discovered by avid learners like yourself.

However, dear reader, remember that continuous learning goes beyond mere theoretical understanding; it necessitates practical application. Engage in hands-on projects that allow you to experiment with various algorithms and techniques firsthand. Delve into coding challenges and collaborative platforms where like-minded individuals converge to share their insights and collectively push boundaries. As you traverse this uncharted territory, never underestimate the power of networking. Attend conferences, seminars, and meetups dedicated to AI enthusiasts who share your fervor for innovation. Surround yourself with brilliant minds whose perspectives can broaden your own horizons while fostering meaningful connections within this vibrant community.

Harnessing the potential of continuous learning involves a multi-faceted approach that extends beyond the confines of traditional education. Engage in interdisciplinary studies, drawing inspiration from fields such as mathematics, statistics, psychology, and even philosophy. By doing so, you will develop a holistic understanding of AI that transcends its technical aspects, enabling you to approach problems with an innovative and well-rounded mindset. In this ever-evolving landscape of AI, it is crucial to remain abreast of the latest advancements and breakthroughs. Stay updated through reputable publications, research papers authored by luminaries in the field, and AI-focused blogs that offer insightful analysis and thought-provoking perspectives. Immerse yourself in the world of AI literature where each page holds untold treasures waiting to be unearthed.

Let us reflect upon the transformative power it bestows upon us. Continuous learning is not merely a means to an end but rather a lifelong companion on our quest for knowledge. It propels us forward, ignites our innate curiosity and pushes us beyond perceived limitations. So dear reader, embrace continuous learning as your compass in this ever-changing realm of artificial intelligence. Revel in its boundless possibilities; for with each step you take towards expanding your horizons, you unravel new dimensions within yourself. In this astonishingly dynamic field where innovation knows no bounds, may your thirst for knowledge be unquenchable and your journey towards mastery be awe-inspiring.

### The Ethical Odyssey of Artificial Intelligence

The world of artificial intelligence is a realm that dazzles and captivates, with its vast potential and boundless possibilities. But as we traverse the uncharted territory of AI, we mustn't forget the crucial role that social responsibility plays in guiding its development. In this chapter, dear readers, we embark on an ethical odyssey through the depths of AI, urging you to join us on this transformative journey.

At the heart of responsible AI lies a profound understanding that it is not simply a tool to be wielded without consequence. No, my friends, it is so much more than that—a creation born from our own ingenuity and imagination. As we delve into the intricacies of ethical AI practices, let us remember that our actions shape its very essence. To embark on this enlightening expedition together, we implore you to actively engage in meaningful discussions surrounding ethical AI practices. Seek out forums where brilliant minds congregate to exchange ideas and challenge conventional notions. It is within these dialogues that innovation thrives and wisdom blossoms.

But dear readers, do not merely confine yourselves to passive observers in these conversations—become advocates for responsible AI development! Let your voices resound like thunderclaps across the technological landscape as you champion principles that safeguard humanity's interests. For we hold within ourselves immense power—the power to mold AI into an instrument of progress rather than one of destruction. As torchbearers for responsible AI development, let us shine light upon three key pillars: transparency, accountability, and inclusivity. These pillars shall guide us through turbulent waters towards a future where humanity flourishes alongside artificial intelligence.

Transparency acts as our compass amid foggy moral dilemmas. We must demand transparency from those who wield the reins of AI—be it governments or corporations—to ensure they are held accountable for their actions. Let there be no cloak-and-dagger maneuvers, no hidden agendas. Only through transparency can we nurture trust and foster a symbiotic relationship between AI and humanity. Accountability, dear readers, is the cornerstone upon which our ethical fortitude is built. We must establish mechanisms to hold those responsible for AI's actions accountable. When AI errs, those who birthed it must shoulder the burden of consequence. Just as parents are responsible for the actions of their children, so too must creators be responsible for their creations.

Lastly, inclusivity beckons us to forge a path where all voices are heard and valued. Let us not succumb to the temptation of exclusivity or favoritism in the development of AI. Instead, let us embrace diversity in all its forms—gender, race, culture—so that AI may truly reflect the collective intelligence of humanity. And so, dear readers, as we conclude this chapter on social responsibility in AI, let your hearts be emboldened by the power you possess—the power to shape a future where artificial intelligence coexists harmoniously with humanity. Join me on this ethical odyssey as we champion transparency, accountability and inclusivity in our pursuit of responsible AI development.

For it is when we open our minds to possibilities beyond what we can fathom that true progress is made. Let us embark on this journey together—one that transcends boundaries and illuminates our path towards a brighter tomorrow—an era where artificial intelligence becomes an ally rather than an adversary. May your conscience guide you as we navigate uncharted waters—a voyage fueled by responsibility and wisdom—a journey that will redefine not only how we perceive artificial intelligence but also how it perceives us.

# Chapter Thirteen

# Glossary of Imporant AI Terms

**AI (Artificial Intelligence):**

The development of computer systems that can perform tasks like understanding language, recognizing patterns, and making decisions, often imitating human intelligence.

**Adversarial Attack:**

A deliberate attempt to trick or confuse an AI model by manipulating the input data to produce incorrect results.

**Algorithm:**

A set of step-by-step instructions that a computer follows to solve a specific problem or perform a task.

**API (Application Programming Interface):**

A set of rules that allows different software applications to communicate with each other.

**Bias:**

Systematic errors in AI models that can lead to unfair or discriminatory outcomes, often influenced by the data used for training.

**ChatGPT Technology:**

A conversational AI technology using models like ChatGPT, designed for interactive and dynamic interactions with users.

**Cloud Computing:**

The delivery of computing services, such as storage and processing, over the internet.

**Computer Vision:**

The ability of computers to interpret and make decisions based on visual data, like images or videos.

**Context Management:**

The capability of an AI model to remember and use information from previous parts of a conversation to provide relevant responses.

**Data:**

Information used by AI systems to learn and make decisions, which can include text, images, numbers, and more.

**Deep Learning:**

A subset of machine learning that involves neural networks with multiple layers, particularly effective for complex tasks.

**Edge AI:**

The deployment of AI models on devices, like smartphones or IoT devices, rather than relying on centralized servers.

**Ethical AI:**

The practice of developing and using AI systems in a fair, transparent, and responsible manner.

**Feature:**

An individual measurable property or characteristic of data used by machine learning algorithms to make predictions.

**General Intelligence:**

The ability of an AI system to understand, learn, and apply knowledge across a wide range of tasks, similar to human intelligence. Achieving general intelligence is a long-term goal in AI research.

**GPU (Graphics Processing Unit):**

A specialized hardware component used to accelerate the training and inference processes of machine learning models.

**Intent Recognition:**

The ability of an AI model to understand the underlying intention or purpose behind user inputs.

### IoT (Internet of Things):

The network of interconnected devices and objects that can communicate and share data. AI is often integrated with IoT to analyze and make decisions based on the data generated by these devices.

### Machine Learning (ML):

A subset of AI that focuses on developing algorithms and models that enable computers to learn from data.

### Machine Translation:

The use of AI to automatically translate text from one language to another. Machine translation models are trained on parallel datasets containing examples of the same text in different languages.

### Midjourney:

An interactive conversational AI platform that incorporates advanced language models like ChatGPT.

### Model:

A representation of a real-world process or system created by a machine learning algorithm based on training data.

### Natural Language Processing (NLP):

A branch of AI that focuses on enabling computers to understand, interpret, and generate human language.

### Prompt Engineering:

The process of crafting specific and clear input prompts to guide AI models in generating desired responses.

### Overfitting:

A common problem in machine learning where a model performs well on the training data but fails to generalize to new, unseen data.

### Quantum Computing:

An area of computing that utilizes the principles of quantum mechanics to perform calculations. Quantum computers have the potential to solve certain problems much faster than classical computers, which could impact AI applications.

### Reinforcement Learning:

A type of machine learning where an algorithm learns by interacting with its environment and receiving feedback.

### Response Generation:

The AI model's ability to generate coherent and contextually relevant responses to user inputs.

### Supervised Learning:

A type of machine learning where the algorithm is trained on labeled data, meaning input data is paired with corresponding output labels.

### Transfer Learning:

A machine learning technique where a model trained on one task is adapted to perform a related task, saving time and resources.

**Unsupervised Learning:**

A type of machine learning where the algorithm is given data without explicit labels, and it discovers patterns and relationships on its own.

**User Input:**

The queries, prompts, or messages provided by users when interacting with AI models.

**UX (User Experience):**

The overall satisfaction and usability of the interaction between users and AI models.

**Validation Set:**

A subset of the data used to evaluate a machine learning model during training. It helps assess the model's performance on new, unseen data.

**Word Embedding:**

A representation of words in a vector space, where words with similar meanings are close to each other. Word embeddings are commonly used in natural language processing tasks.

**XGBoost:**

An open-source machine learning library that provides an efficient and scalable implementation of the gradient boosting framework. It is often used for classification and regression tasks.